# IT TAKES TIME TO LOVE

BY

## HUGH STEVEN

Scripture quotations in this volume are from the Living Bible, Copyright © 1971 Tyndale House Publishers, Wheaton, Illinois 60187.


Other Wycliffe books by Hugh Steven:

Manuel
Miracles in Mexico (Hefley/Steven)
You Eat Bananas
Night of the Long Knives
The Measure of Greatness
It Takes Time to Love


First Printing, 1974
Second Printing, 1976


© 1974 WYCLIFFE BIBLE TRANSLATORS, INC.


Printed in the United States of America

Library of Congress Catalog Card Number 74-84490

Especially for
the praying and supporting friends
of Wycliffe workers
in the Philippines
and Vietnam

# TABLE OF CONTENTS

## APPRECIATION

## PREFACE

## PART I

## PART II

## PREFACE

# APPRECIATION

Because so many of my Philippine and Vietnam Wycliffe colleagues helped with factual and anecdotal material, I hesitate a recital of names. However, I do express appreciation to Philippine Branch Director Morris Cottle for his warm cooperation, and the same to Associate Director Daniel Weaver. It was he who provided me Joseph France, an excellent JAARS pilot and cordial compeer.

I am grateful also to Elizabeth Stevens who allowed her article "Feeding of the 400" (previously published in *Translation*) to be used in this anthology.

And to Joanne Shetler, Len Newell, Ed and Jackie Ruch, and Dick and Betty Elkins for sharing their lives and stories.

I express the same appreciation to Vietnam Director Dick Watson and his wife, Sandy, for their hospitality and help. To Ken and Marilyn Smith and each member of the Vietnam branch I met during my visit. I have the warmest of memories and thank God for every remembrance of your courage, love, and fidelity to Bible translation.

Lastly to my wife Norma who continues to be my strong right arm in our cooperative ministry of writing for the glory of Jesus Christ our Lord.

Hugh Steven

# PREFACE

Someone once said, "The gospel is Jesus Christ, who He is, what He has done, and how He can be known in personal experience."

John the Apostle said, "When people know Christ in a personal way they become His bride — the Church." According to Revelation, the Church is an integrated body made up of every tribe, tongue, people, and nation who will one day stand before the King of kings to sing His praises and do His will.

It is the goal of every Wycliffe worker along with his praying and financial backers at home to be the Holy Spirit's instrument to bring this about. Since Wycliffe first began in 1935, there are representatives of more than 600 ethnic peoples from 26 countries who are receiving parts or all of the New Testament and now have the privilege of taking part in that celestial acclamation.

But spiritual rebirth for these people has usually been long and hard because the battle over men's souls remains as it always has, a fight against the unseen satanic princes of darkness.

The following stories illustrate Paul's words in Ephesians 6:12, that we wrestle not against flesh and blood but against principles, against powers, against spiritual wickedness in high places. The stories are true and show God at work in a segment of Wycliffe's world-wide ministry of unfolding His secret plan. What is that secret? This is the secret: that Christ in your hearts is your only hope of glory (Colossians 1:27b).

PART ONE

IT TAKES TIME TO LOVE

# CHAPTER ONE

## THE BOOK'S NOT DONE

It was mid-April 1968. The rice terraces of the Balangao people in the northern Philippine Island of Luzon were filled with heavy-headed pea green rice stalks just a few weeks away from harvest.

Joanne (Jo) Shetler, a vivacious Bible translator for the Balangaos, paused from her work and looked out through the shuttered window of her 10 by 18 foot plank house.

"It's not right," she thought, "that so many of the Balangaos in this beautiful valley are still held in control by Satan and his demonic hordes." Then with a strong impassioned plea Jo prayed out loud: "Father, more Balangaos must come to know You and understand You created all this. Please, please, Father, do something to show these people You have more power than the evil spirits!"

Jo wanted to pray longer but was stopped by a bone-chilling scream. "Oh no," she thought, "not again! It sounds like Benito's son-in-law."

Jo arrived in the Philippines in 1962 with a feverish desire to translate a New Testament and see the establishment of a strong indigenous church. Shortly after her arrival Jo learned about the Balangaos. It didn't matter to her the Balangao area was considered dangerous and before an airstrip could be built would require a two-day hike over steep lung-splitting mountains. It seemed to her and her then partner, Anne Fetzer, this was the place God was leading them to do a work for Him.

But during her first five years there were only two Balangao believers — both women. During those beginning years Jo slowly and sometimes painfully learned what it meant to be a translator and a woman among a proud isolated ethnic people.

Several months before Jo and Anne arrived, a Wycliffe survey team visited the Balangaos and asked if they would allow translators to learn their language. The people were overjoyed with the prospect of Americans living with them. But when Jo and Anne arrived, the Balangaos threw up their hands and said, "Not women!" Even Ama, who later adopted Jo and Anne into his family, lamented the translators were women. "If only you were men," he said, "you would then learn the ways of our people faster and better."

Because the Balangaos were headhunters, it wasn't safe for women to live alone. Therefore, Jo and Anne became Ama's daughters and he became their Balangao father. Unknown to the girls this solemn pronouncement meant this man and his extended family would defend their lives and honor to the death if it ever became necessary.

For two full years Jo and Anne studied the Balangao language, made friends, worked on beginning translation, sutured wounds, and delivered babies. The phrase "Since you came our women

Adroit and explosive mountain Balangao and Ifugao peoples of northern Luzon have for three thousand years built and tilled an enormous network of irrigated rice terraces.

don't die in childbirth," became a happy
watchword among the Balangaos.

Then Anne left to begin a new assignment —
marriage. Shortly after Anne left, Ama said, "From
now on you must eat your meals with us. If you
eat alone you'll become lonely and if you get
lonely you'll leave."

For six years, from 1964 to 1971 with one year
out in 1967 for furlough, Jo ate her meals with her
Balangao family. "And," said Jo, "I told Ama the
gospel every time I ate with him but he didn't seem
to understand what I was saying."

In 1967 Jo returned to her native Paso Robles,
California for furlough with the burden of
challenging her church and Christian friends to
pray for the Balangaos. She told how the Lord had
given two believers. Tekla was the first — a small,
friendly woman, who, when they first arrived,
asked why they had come to live with her people.
"We have come to put God's Word in a book so
you can read it," they told her. With great longing
Tekla said, "I wish I could know God." And when
they explained how she could, she believed.

Jo told about Andrea, another woman who
believed when they worked together translating the
gospel of Mark. "And now just before I left the
Philippines," continued Jo, "many of the Balangaos told me they wanted to believe but were
afraid."

Jo explained the Balangaos wanted to stop the
expensive sacrificing of their farm animals to the
spirits but were desperately afraid of the spirits'
power. "What are you going to do when your child
is sick," said one man with a great look of

hopelessness in his eyes. "Stop sacrificing and let him die?"

"Pray that God will show Himself strong on behalf of the Balangaos," said Jo, "and also that they will want to meet and study the translated Scriptures."

Jo returned to the Philippines and her Balangao village in 1968, two days after Andrea's first and only child died. "Oh God," prayed Jo, "why? What is the purpose in the death of this child? You know how long Andrea prayed to You for a child and how happy she was when You answered."

If Andrea had doubts about God's sovereignty, no one knew it. "When people of the village come to comfort me," she said to Jo, "please be here to tell them about God and where my little baby is now."

Not only did Jo talk to them, she showed and explained the Scriptures from the newly published Gospel of Mark. At this point the people began to express an immediate interest and wanted to continue studying the Scriptures.

"Out of this sad, 'premature' death of Andrea's baby," said Jo, "came the beginning of our first Bible study and public meetings."

A few weeks later Jo accompanied Ama to the dentist to help him buy a set of dentures. During the few days it took to get the work done, they began work on First John.

"I gave him a carbon copy of the book," said Jo, "and we started to go over it verse by verse. Suddenly for the first time during all the years I had explained the Gospel, I saw his interest become intense."

"Why, these are good words!" Ama said excitedly. "People would believe this if they could just hear it."

At that point Jo realized more profoundly than ever the Balangaos wouldn't believe the Gospel merely on the strength of her own words. When Ama believed Jo understood in a new way that the language of faith is the translated Scriptures in the vernacular.

After Ama believed he immediately assumed the responsibility for the Bible study and evangelism of his village. The first Sunday after they returned from the dentist, Ama rounded up a number of people and brought them to Jo's house for a Bible study. Over and over again they asked where people first came from, why man was separated from God, and how men get back to God.

Patiently week by week Jo answered their questions, taught them gospel songs, and read and reread the translated Balangao Scriptures. And one by one they said, "Yes we will follow God."

Then it happened. Just as soon as a person said he wanted to follow God and stopped sacrificing to the evil spirits, everything seemed to go wrong.

The new believer usually experienced an abnormal amount of sickness, difficulties, and premature death in his family. Terminal cancer was diagnosed in the wife of one man who showed only beginning interest in believing. Another new believer's sixteen-year-old daughter almost bled to death as she gave birth to her first child. To Jo and the Balangao believers this was clearly the work of evil spirits retaliating over the loss of power and control. Jo's fervent constant prayer was that God would defeat the evil spirits before the eyes of the

Balangaos. Often in the middle of the night, or as she did on that April day in 1968, Jo shouted her prayer to God that He would bring glory to His name and defeat the spirits.

"Juami (Jo's Balangao name)!" screamed Benito's son-in-law, a new believer. "Come quickly! Benito's son is dying!"

Skipping expertly over the large gray cobblestones of her village, Jo reached Benito's house in record time. Inside she saw a room full of horrified people watching the six-year-old boy convulse on the floor. Standing over him, a woman witch doctor shook and quivered like a person with a hyperactive case of Parkinson's Disease (characteristic of a demon-possessed person). In one corner the boy's mother, supported by friends, screamed hysterically at the witch doctor. "We have four pigs! We have ten chickens! We have rice! What do you want?"

Then just as the spirits began speaking through the witch doctor, Jo screamed, "Get out!" But the people yelled back, "No wait!" To the horror of the people in the room, Jo again yelled for the witch doctor to leave. Unknown to Jo, the Balangaos *never* interrupted the spirits when they talked through a possessed person.

Then as Jo gathered up the boy to take him to her house, she called out, "Don't any of you be frightened. You'll see God is stronger than the spirits! He won't let the boy die."

"Okay, God," said Jo under her breath, "here's Your chance!"

By the time Jo and the boy reached her house his convulsions stopped. After praying she examined him and found nothing wrong. But the boy said his neck hurt.

"Why is your neck sore?" asked Jo.

"Because," answered the boy, "I saw the spirits coming for me. They tried to cut my back with their bolos (machetes) but I screamed and fell on the floor."

Jo again prayed over the boy and with his mother when she took him home. "Don't be afraid," said Jo as she left. "Just watch and see how God will keep your boy alive."

And God did! The boy lived and the family was eventually released from the paralyzing fear of spirit reprisals. But it took prayer, the reading of Scripture, and Jo and Tekla's daily counseling visits to reassure the family that God could be trusted.

Returning from one of her visits, Jo stopped to see the old witch doctor who had been demon-possessed in Benito's house. In true Christian love Jo apologized for her rude treatment of her.

"I am sorry, too," said the old witch doctor, "but the spirits make me do it."

"You know," answered Jo, "you don't have to be controlled by the spirits if you don't want to. God is stronger and He will protect you and can even send the spirits away if you ask for His help."

"But," said the old woman, "what do you tell God when you ask Him to send them away?"

Carefully Jo taught her a simple prayer asking God in Jesus' name to protect her.

The following morning Jo and Tekla began working on translation but were interrupted by vigorous knocking on the back door. It was the old witch doctor. Jo smiled but before she could open her mouth to welcome her, the woman began to scream in wild-eyed terror.

"Send them away! Send them away! They've been kicking and pinching me all night!"

Jo was about to ask for an explanation when the woman continued. "It all happened when I tried to pray that prayer you taught me."

Jo, who in a moment of high courage had acted bravely a few days earlier, was now, in her own words, scared. Quickly she called for Tekla to come and pray.

"After we prayed," said Jo, "the old woman seemed better and left." But later that afternoon Jo's door burst open and the old witch doctor who always used a cane actually *ran* screaming through Jo's door.

Jo could hardly believe what she was seeing. The old woman was shaking with a shake characteristic of demon possession. Perspiration ran down her face and she was doubled over in pain.

"They're killing me! They're killing me!" she screamed. "Send them away!"

"It just looked like something was stabbing her," said Jo.

Jo and Tekla again prayed as they had done earlier, with the old woman trying to repeat their words. Halfway through the prayer, Jo stopped. "Your problem," said Jo gently, "is that you're not God's child. You need to repent of your sins and ask God to make you His child because God protects His own children."

To Jo's surprise the old woman didn't wait for her to begin praying as she had done before. She just looked up and shouted, "God, it is true. I am wicked and in my old age I come to you; just a remnant of me left. But now I want you to make me Yours; Yours only and nobody else's."

When she said, "Make me Yours and nobody else's," she immediately stopped shaking. The pain stopped and she stood in the middle of the floor — weak, quiet, like the great silence after a violent storm.

"You are now a child of God," said Jo. "The angels in heaven are happy and are rejoicing because of your faith in Jesus. This is a great miracle. Let's prove God's power and ask Him to give you a good night's sleep." Jo knew the old woman and others like her were constantly disturbed from sleep by tormenting spirits.

The following morning, her curiosity about to boil over, Jo ran down the hill to visit the old woman. "It was a moment I'll never forget," said Jo. "She was ecstatically happy. She had slept all night!"

Still curious, Jo asked if the spirits had in any way bothered her. "Yes," said the woman, "but when they came I asked God to send them away and He did. Then I went back to sleep."

After Tekla, Andrea, Ama, the old witch doctor, and others believed and didn't die as most Balangaos expected, a new sense of hope spread over the village. In the past other witch doctors had tried to stop sacrificing and were killed by the spirits. Now they began to realize the spirits could be defeated; they didn't have to obey them and sacrifice their animals each time illness occurred. The icy fear of spirit reprisal was replaced with the warm confidence of God's Holy Spirit.

Typical of the many who believed was one old man who after realizing the old witch doctor wasn't going to die, came to talk with Ama. "You know God better than I do," he said, "would you ask Him if He would please list my name too?"

As others had their names *listed*, the small Bible study that Ama held each week in Jo's house exploded to a four-hour Sunday service with sometimes over a hundred people. Jo now had a different kind of prayer request with which to challenge her home constituency.

When the evil spirit crisis came, Jo asked her friends at home to join her in earnest prayer for God to defeat the spirits. And He did. As time went on she prayed with the same intensity for God to do something that would teach the Balangao believers to pray. This need for serious prayer became especially important to Jo when she returned to the village after a short absence. The Balangao believers told her they had frightened off a plague of locusts by chants, screams, and hitting gongs. Jo was disappointed.

"Did your ancestors ever frighten away the locusts by chanting and hitting gongs?" asked Jo.

"No," they said.

"Then why give credit to screams and gongs," said Jo, "when this was clearly the hand of God protecting your crops?"

"Oh, God," prayed Jo later, "You've got to do something to teach these people to pray. I don't care how or what You do. Teach these people to pray at any price." That price almost became her life.

On April 15, 1971, Jo began a prayer newsletter to her friends at home calling them to pray specifically about the growing pains of the new Balangao Church.

"Dear folks at home," she began, "our 'church' service begins each Sunday from 8:00 to 12:00 a.m. The children come first to sing. Then about seventy adults somehow squeeze into my 10' by 18' room and take their place to study the translated Scripture. There are others who stand outside. I don't need to tell you how desperately we need a church."

Jo also wrote about the need for special prayer regarding the strengthening of believers. "Evil is so devious," she wrote. "It captures the believers in unexpected ways."

There were other items of praise and concern Jo wanted to share but she never finished. Halfway through her letter she was asked, along with JAARS pilot Bill Powell, to act as interpreter and guide aboard a big U.S. military transport helicopter. A Dr. Robespierre Lim had asked for U.S. military assistance to transport a large quantity of cement and building materials to a new hospital site in the mountains above Jo's village.

Material for the hospital was loaded in Bagabag, Wycliffe's northern base of operations. Bill Powell, the crew, Dr. Lim, Domingo (a Balangao), and Jo boarded the helicopter in happy spirits.

They made the twenty minute flight to Jo's village without incident. Then something went wrong. All of a sudden they were lower than their landing site. They saw a betelnut tree lose its top and they knew they were going to crash.

Bill grabbed the iron plating behind the copilot's seat and hung on. The betelnut tree had thrown the rotor out of balance and they were going down quickly. Somehow the pilot guided the stricken craft into the only spot in town where there were no houses. It was a deep ravine.

The helicopter struck hard and immediately turned over, but the rotor kept turning, thrashing and shaking the heliocopter like a terrier shaking a rat.

"I kept my eyes closed against the cloud of cement that was flying in all directions," said Bill, "but opened them every few seconds to see if I was still alive."

Bill tore out the plexiglass and slid down the plane. With one good arm (a sharp piece of 1½" steel had pierced his other forearm) he started up the steep bank followed by the pilot and copilot. But then Bill suddenly remembered Jo, Dr. Lim, and Domingo still trapped inside and to his horror he saw the tail section was on fire.

Scrambling back down the bank, Bill tried to climb into the plane but his bad arm hindered his climbing up to the opening in the windshield. Seeing the gushing fuel, the pilots screamed for Bill and the Balangaos who had gathered, to run. "It's going to explode!" they yelled.

Bill realized the immediate danger of the explosion but called out to the Balangaos, "Juami, Domingo, and Dr. Lim are inside!"

When the Balangaos heard that Jo was trapped inside, they immediately formed a bucket brigade to quench the fire with water and dirt. After the fire was under control, others jumped up on the plane and began throwing out kegs of nails and cement in a frantic effort to reach Jo and the others.

Jo, who had been knocked unconscious and was literally buried under tons of cement and nail kegs, revived when she heard shouts of "fire" and Balangaos calling her name.

"I was in a hopeless upside down position," said Jo later, "with cement caked in my nose, mouth, and eyes. I could barely breathe. The only thing I could move was the fingers on my left hand. When I heard the shouts of fire and knew I couldn't get out, I wondered if this was how I was to die.

"Then I felt people walking over me and after what seemed a very long time, I felt two strong hands around my ankles."

After Bill saw Jo being removed from the plane, he ran to her house an hour away over rice terraces and radioed news of the crash to the Bagabag base. When he returned to the crash site he discovered the sad news that young Dr. Lim had been killed. Miraculously Domingo and the crewmen all escaped serious injury.

But Jo was in serious condition. Tenderly the Balangaos carried her back to her house on a pole stretcher and washed and changed her clothes. They were frightened by her severe head wounds and tried to stop the bleeding by suturing one of the deep cuts.

Jo knew her ribs and collarbone were broken and it was later revealed she had a collapsed lung. But her concern was for her eyes. Blackened by the cement, they were beginning to blister and bug out like eyes on a great toad. She knew a military rescue helicopter would come in the morning but wondered how she would survive the long night. The lime in the cement burned her eyes like a searing fire. "God," she prayed, "I just can't be blind. How can I be a translator and not have eyesight?"

All night Jo insisted the Balangaos repeatedly wash out her eyes with the cold mountain water. Many were frightened of hurting her but they did as she asked. It was later revealed the water saved her eyesight.

News of the crash spread like wildfire and before the night was over more than 200 Balangaos gathered to pray for God to save her life.

"You can't let Juami die," they prayed, "because the Book's not done."

"The night was long and painful," said Jo, "but it was without question the most thrilling night of my life. The Balangaos were actually praying on their own for God to do something for them.

Jo left the following morning and the Balangaos continued to pray every night. "God, You can't let her die. She can't die. The Book's not done."

And Jo didn't die. Six weeks later she walked back into her village and into the arms and lives of the Balangao people. Not because she's braver than you, but because the Book's not done!

# CHAPTER TWO

## LOVE NEEDS TIME

The island of Coron in the Palawan chain is one
of hundreds of coral and limestone islands that
make up the archipelago of the Philippine Sulu
Sea. Lying south of China and east of India, Coron,
Palawan, Mindanao, Cebu, Jolo, and others
received explorers, marauding Malay and Indone-
sian pirates, and Chinese merchants as early as 200
B.C.

Primarily interested in trade, the Chinese found
the abruptly rising cliffs, sea walls, and caves of
Coron ideal nesting places for great colonies of
southeast Asia swifts. They pursued these tireless
flyers not for their eggs or flesh, but their nests
which are made almost entirely from the swift's
saliva. This, when it hardens, looks like a milky
isinglass saucer and is used to make bird's nest
soup. Today, thirteen centuries later, the 5000
petite, good-looking Kalamian Tagbanwa people of
Coron still collect the swift's saliva-hardened nests
for the world's soup bowls.

Less interested in gastronomical delights, two
great East Indian empires of antiquity from Java
and Sumatra — the Scri-Vijaya (A.D. 800-1377)
and Majapahit (A.D. 1293-1478) — made lasting
cultural, religious, and linguistic impressions on the

The Philippines has over five million ethnic minority peoples who speak 120 different languages.

Philippines. Then in the late 14th century, Islam boiled out of the Malay penninsula and swept across Mindanao and the Sulu Sea like a prairie grass fire. Reaching as far north as Manila, the *fire* was arrested by Filipine discoverer Ferdinand Magellan who subsequently fell in battle by warriors under the explosive leadership of Lapu-Lapu, heroic tribal chieftain from the Island of Mactan.

Later, Ruy Lopez de Villalobos (who named the Philippines after King Philip of Spain) and the Augustinian friar, Fray Andres de Urdaneta, succeeded in establishing a foothold that led after much bloodshed and fighting to pacification and conversion to Catholicism. The Moros (name given to Muslims by the Spanish) of Mindanao and Sulu, however, successfully resisted Spanish influence and domination from the northern Island. Today Mindanao and the islands of the Sulu Sea remain predominantly Muslim.

Since then, Filipine history has been studded with turmoil, romance, and tragedy with foreign traders, entrepreneurs, and world governments (including the United States) vying for control of its land, resources, and people.

This historical association with Indonesia, China, Spain, Arabia, Europe, and Mexico blended with Malay stock to produce one of the world's most beautiful people. As its blood was mixed, so were its languages. Almost 40 million people scattered over 115,707 square miles speak eight major languages with eight different life styles and value systems. In addition, the 120 different languages are spoken by the country's five million ethnic minority people.

It was into this mosaic of culture and history that Wycliffe Bible translators began work in the Philippines in 1953. Tactical bases of operations were established in northern Luzon and southern Mindinao, administrative offices and living accomodations for staff and visitors in Manila, air strips opened, new workers allocated, and language surveys conducted along with linguistic and Bible translation workshops.

The Philippine branch has participated in community development, been a good neighbor, and encouraged and conducted writer's workshops and linguistic training courses for Filipinos. In recognition of this, it was elected to win the 1973 Ramon Magsaysay Award (equal in honor to the Nobel Peace Prize) for "international understanding and its inspired outreach to non-literate tribespeople." But central to all this activity and more has been the goal of a translated New Testament and on-going indigenous church among all ethnic minorities and language groups, and many translators are seeing the Holy Spirit work in their areas to bring this about.

But some like Ed and Jackie Ruch who work with the Tagbanwa people of Coron, Palawan have seen only minimal results.

I waited with Ed and Jackie one balmy afternoon in a small airport in Mindanao and listened to Jackie admonish me in her broad Philadelphia accent not to write only success stories. "Our area has seen only two Tagbawan people come to know the Lord in fifteen years," she said.

On the plane flying out over the sparkling Sulu Sea on my way back to Manila, I reflected on

Jackie's statement. As I did, I remembered an earlier statement by Philippine Director Morris Cottle. "I see the church as something Christ brings into being and over which we as translators have no way of plotting how the Holy Spirit will work in a given area."

Pressed by home constituencies for results, some translators become discouraged when, in the accustomed tradition of American speed and efficiency, churches do not spring up like mushrooms after a spring rain. In some cases they do. But constituents must remember a translator faces two almost impregnable foes — one, human nature set against change and the concept of Jesus Christ as an authority in their lives. And two, the contending not against flesh and blood but against principalities and powers, the world rulers of this present darkness, the spiritual hosts of wickedness in high places, and the kingdom of evil. As soldiers in the army of God properly armed with the weapons and equipment to withstand the real enemy of man, the translator (and all Christians) must battle against "huge numbers of wicked spirits in the spirit world" (Ephesians 6:12b).

To the world and inexperienced, the weapons all Christians must use look frail and ineffective. But God says truth, love of righteousness, faith in His Son Jesus Christ, and prayer, are the only weapons strong enough to destroy Satan's stronghold over men.

While human nature is naturally set against God, it does possess a universal vulnerability. Man's Achilles' heel is his limitless need for love. But love needs time to incubate and grow. And it takes time for a translator to learn the perplexing array of

Angelina — God's first fruit among the Tagbanwas.

sounds and idiosyncrasies that make up language. Yet learning a language well enough to communicate meaningfully is not enough. Qualities of trust and belief need to be established between translator and people.

The translator knows that people who live in isolated communities, dominated by demonic activity and long historical cultural traditions, present a set of evangelistic problems unrelatable to home constituents. It's a truism that vital things take a long time to grow. Therefore, in spite of the heavy forces of evil, indifference, and/or misunderstanding, the translator willingly spends the necessary years translating a New Testament because he knows this to be the most effective and permanent contribution he can make to church planting, spiritual growth, and evangelism.

The Gospel seed must be planted, watered, nurtured, and given a chance to grow. And when the time is ripe (a time determined by God), the Holy Spirit will bring the Church of God into being.

Ed and Jackie Ruch know this and look forward in faith to the time God will work in the hearts of the Tagbanwa people of Coron. In the meanwhile they continue to translate the Scriptures and point to Kudul and his sister Angelina as signs of God's first fruit.

In her late teens, Angelina (Angie) is a compact petite charmer with skin the color of polished mahogany and teeth whiter than a Pepsodent toothpaste ad. She lived and worked closely with Ed and Jackie for six years before she came *close* to Jesus. Her brother Kudul, the first believer among the Tagbanwas, warned Ed how difficult it would be.

"Uncle," said Kudul, "these things we teach are new to my people. Their thoughts are very much satisfied with what they are already holding on to."

Kudul was right. His people are very much satisfied with their life style, or so it seems. The Ruches seldom sense the slightest outward indication that the widespread promiscuity, lying, stealing, and pseudo pleasures affect the Tagbanwa's conscience. Under Satan's dominance, Tagbanwas don't seem to feel the ropes and gloom that bind and suffocate their spiritual freedom.

And Angie wasn't too different from her contemporaries. Her easy-going charm made her a natural candidate for all that Tagbanwas thought to be part of their birthright.

Then, slowly at first, Jackie began to notice a slight change in Angie's attitude. The change came during a time when they were translating at a translation workshop along with other translators and their language helpers. As Ed worked on Acts he shared each morning after breakfast what he had translated the day before.

Observing her growing interest in Scriptures, Ed decided one morning to ask Angie to pray before they ate. To his and Jackie's surprise she not only prayed and thanked God for the food but asked God to help Ed translate and teach His Word, "because Your Word is like pure water to drink."

After that initial prayer, Ed and Jackie noticed a change in the content of her prayers. She began to thank God for providing a path for sinful people to walk on so they could get back and come close to

God. But she always ended by saying, "If only I could find that path and get on it so I could come close to God."

Several days later, after listening to another translator's language helper tell how he had "come close to God," Ed asked Angie to explain what he had said. To his surprise Angie began using Tagbanwa vocabulary he had never heard before. To his further surprise she burst into tears when Ed asked her to explain what they meant.

"I have been trying to come close to God for a long time," she sobbed, "but my sins feel so heavy and seem to block my way and I don't know what to do about it."

Carefully Ed explained again how Jesus had come to take her sins out of the way. There were more sobs and Angie remarked that because she had sinned so much she doubted that Jesus would accept her the way she was. "Jesus says in John 6:37," said Ed, "that whoever will come to Him He will never cast them away." But Angie still continued to weep and Ed felt he should leave her alone.

Later that evening while Ed was studying in the library at the translation center, Angie and Jackie came in. "Angie has something she wants to talk to you about," said Jackie.

With characteristic warmth and tenderness Ed asked Angie what it was. But as she began Angie again burst into sobbing tears. "Her whole body seemed to convulse," said Ed later, "and then after a while she began to explain."

"During the six years I have lived and worked with you," she said, "I only pretended to listen to what you and Auntie were saying about Jesus. And

when you read the Scriptures I would not let it
penetrate my mind. At times I felt bad because I
did this. And sometimes I could not even understand why I did. Then during these days as we have
been reading the Scriptures every morning I began
to think differently and truly wanted to come
close to God. But each time I try I feel the
heaviness of my sin. It feels like a big piece of
wood that has been soaking in the ocean for a long
time."

As Ed again related Scriptures and promises of
God, Jackie assured Angie that when she confessed
her sin to God, He would forgive and forget every
sin she ever committed.

For almost an hour and a half Ed and Jackie
talked and encouraged Angie to tell God all about
her life. And then from the depths of her soul
Angie openly confessed all to God. Angie's confes-
sion surprised the Ruches. Not because she frankly
told about her promiscuity, lying, and malicious
gossip against her sister-in-law, but because it was
so un-Tagbanwa to be repentant about such things.

After listing each one, Jackie suggested to Angie
that she ask God to "please erase it." And Angie
did. Then she asked Ed what she should do next.
"Tell God," said Ed, "that you know Jesus died
for the sins you mentioned and that you want to
turn yourself completely over to Him."

"Dear Jesus," prayed Angie, "I want you now to
be my boss."

In the days that followed it became absolutely
clear that the Holy Spirit had truly transcended
Tagbanwa cultural barriers. In a testimony given to
the washer ladies at the translation center, Angie's

words about her new relationship to Christ flowed out with deep meaning and sincerity.

Unusually astute, Angie expressed concern for her return to Coron. "I know the kinds of temptations that will be there for me," she said. "Please pray that I will be strong and not give in."

Angie and Kudul have determined to live their lives differently. In so doing they have won the greatest of all spiritual battles — emerging by faith in Christ out of the kingdom of darkness and evil into the kingdom of light and eternal life. This with its potential to heal the human spirit and make all things new is without question the most explosive and staggering of all historical events to come to Coron — the beginning of Christ's Church.

# CHAPTER THREE

## WHAT HAPPENS WHEN IT HAPPENS?

Eight hundred years before Christ, southern Mexico experienced the mathematical and architectural wizardry of the sharp-nosed almond-eyed Mayas. Northwest Africa had the Songhai people who founded Timbuktu, the sophisticated city and seat of learning and government. And the people of the Philippine Islands point to the adroit and explosive mountain Ifugao and Balangao headhunters of northern Luzon who for three thousand years have built and tilled an enormous network of irrigated rice terraces, the walls of which if placed end to end would reach halfway around the earth. They remain a living monument of incredible engineering skill and practical mastery over an impossible environmental condition.

Yet for all their skill and freedom to create in the natural world, most ethnic minorities of Luzon, Mindanao, Palawan, the Visayas, and other islands of the Philippines, do not enjoy the free gift of spiritual liberty. Most live their lives haunted with the fear of offending and being permanently possessed by evil spirits.

When handsome auburn-haired Len Newell with his petite energetic wife, Doreen, began work among the 1500 Ifugaos in the village of Batad in

1961, they discovered many Ifugaos bound in the insidious clutch of satanic powers.

Babot was two when Len and Doreen came to Batad. Like most Ifugao children she was shy, sometimes happy, always dirty, and most always wore a tattered dress three sizes too large. In her short twenty-four months of life, little Babot had suffered the searing pain of dysentery and pneumonia. In both cases she almost died. The village pagan priests *understood* Babot's problem. Her dead grandmother was angry because the family did not offer her enough food and wine. When she became hungry she seized Babot's soul as a ransom until the family offered sufficient rice, wine, and chickens.

Only after the village priests brought out Grandmother's bones, offered the appropriate sacrifices, and implored the spirits to relinquish Babot's soul, did Babot live. And after she became well again, Babot's father was confident the gods would not try to rob them of their only child. "After all," he reasoned, "the spirits have already taken our four other children."

But one night several weeks later Babot woke her mother and father with a persistent cough. They examined her and discovered she was gasping for breath and burning with fever. Then without warning Babot began to convulse wildly. "Quick!" shouted Babot's mother. "Get the priests! The gods are angry and must be appeased."

The family's few chickens were immediately sacrificed. But Babot didn't respond and two more priests were called. With the father they formed a circle around an altar on which sat a jar of pungent rice wine. (According to custom Babot's mother

Shy little Babot was two when translators Len and Doreen Newell first came to work among the Batad Ifugao people. In her short twenty-four months of life, Babot suffered the searing pain of dysentery and pneumonia. In both cases she almost died.

was not allowed to be present during the sacrificing.) Then sixteen chickens were ceremoniously given to the gods.

But as darkness fell, Babot's little body still burned with fever. "The gods are extremely angry," said the priest. "If the child is to live we must sacrifice pigs."

Without a moment's hesitation Babot's father left to find a buyer for his rice terraces — an inheritance passed down from father to son for over two thousand years!

After a long search Babot's father found a buyer and sold his only means of livelihood for a fraction of its true value. With the money he bought six pigs and brought them to the priests. Hardly understanding what was happening, the father stood dumb as the priests slaughtered the pigs one by one and with monotonous chantings, implored the wicked spirits to accept the soul of the pigs as a substitute for that of the child's.

But after four days of sacrificing, Babot lay glassy-eyed on her straw mat in the corner of the one-room hut still burning with fever, her every breath an agonizing effort.

"Why don't you go to the Americans for help?" suggested someone to the father. "Unthinkable," said the priest. "If the gods are angry now, how much more they will be if the parents allow foreigner's medicine to be given to the child. No," continued the priest, "the sacrifices must continue. We need more pigs."

Already destitute, the family sold their last possession — a tall, glazed porcelain rice wine jar, a Ming dynasty heirloom beyond monetary value. And like the rice terraces, it had been passed down from generation to generation. Nevertheless it was sold. Life was more important than an heirloom. And four more pigs were purchased.

In the late afternoon of the seventh day, the monotonous chanting inside the grass-roofed hut suddenly stopped. Anxiously the mother fixed her eyes on the door. Finally if opened and the weary father stepped out. Babot was dead!

The following morning the father carried the lifeless little bundle over the rice terraces and up the side of a mountain to a tiny shallow grave. Later, towards evening, the family discovered Grandfather missing. They found him with his bolo knife beside him, keeping a silent vigil over the grave. When they asked why he was there he declared through tears that life was cruel and meaningless with no rewards but suffering, heartache, and death. "Perhaps," he said, determining to end his own life, "in that far-off land of death the gods will be more kind."

Watching as outsiders but sorrowing as friends, two things became crystal clear to the Newells. First they would double their efforts to master the Ifugao language, and second, God's Word must be translated into the Ifugao language at all cost. "So," said Len, "they might experience the truth of John 8:32 and be free indeed!"

When Len and Doreen did learn the language they discovered the Ifugaos believed all sickness and natural phenomena to be controlled and manipulated by evil spirits. Through chants and sacrifices, the Ifugaos were in daily communication with a pantheon of spirits which they knew intimately by name, a practice which caused a suffocating economical and psychological drain on the Ifugaos.

For almost ten years Len and Doreen battered this iron-clad, often frightening system with Christian love, determination, and creativity. In a land where mountains rise up and down like teeth on a rip saw, pasture and grazing land is almost non-existent. To help meet the demand for protein, Len instituted a successful chicken farm program. Doreen began sewing classes, Len trained typists to assist him in typing translated Scriptures, and together they created an indigenous medical clinic.

But more important, the Newells became respected friends and translators of the good news of Jesus Christ into the Batad Ifugao language. Yet for all this, the Newells were not satisfied. The few Ifugaos who did believe were not growing and the air of depression which comes from sacrificial spirit worship was ominously heavy in many of their lives. Len's administrative duties often kept him occupied in Manila on Wycliffe business, away from the translation desk. When Scriptures were finally translated, printing and technical difficulties created further roadblocks.

"It wasn't until 1969," said Len, "that we were able to publish and distribute large quantities of translated Ifugao Scriptures. Then as the Ifugaos read and discussed the translated Scriptures in the quiet privacy of their own block-type houses, things began to happen."

"You know, sir," said an Ifugao believer to Len one day, "this Scripture you translate is very, very strange."

"How so?" said Len.

"Since I've understood it," he said, "I've found I can't do things I used to. Last week I was walking on a trail by some sugar cane. I wanted to cut a piece and eat it but something told me I shouldn't do this because it was a form of stealing."

This was the first indication Len had that the Lord was working. Then he began to notice people discussing the deep questions of immorality, murder, and drunkenness, comparing what the Scriptures taught with what the village elders said.

But this new freedom to challenge the system meant a severe testing for some. One of these was Ilat, Len's friend, principal language helper, energetic colporteur, and lay preacher. For several months Ilat had listened to the taunts of the priests during his baptism services, warning him the spirits would not stand so many Ifugaos breaking away from the sacrificial system to follow Jesus Christ. Ilat knew their threats were serious and made special efforts to arm himself by memorizing Scripture, never dreaming the attack would come not to him, but his wife.

The day after his wife Inyap had given birth, Ilat came to Len and told him she was hemorrhaging slightly. After Len gave her a vitamin K injection he told Ilat to keep Inyap quiet and lying down.

Early the following morning, Len awoke to Ilat's excited banging on the door. "My wife is bleeding badly!" he said.

"Is she in bed?" asked Len.

"No, she got up," said Ilat.

"Well, get her lying down and I'll be right over."

Fifteen minutes later Len arrived and found an almost unbelievable large pool of blood on the ground that had dripped down through the split bamboo floor of the stilt house. "Look," said Len, "we've got to get your wife to a doctor in a hurry or she'll bleed to death. As soon as my radio schedule comes on at 7:15 I'll radio the Far Eastern Gospel Crusade's clinic at Banaue. In the meantime you find some carriers and I'll make a stretcher."

At 7:15 Len made contact with Far Eastern's clinic at Banaue but was unable to talk to the doctor. With his precise Canadian diction he related the problem to the operator and asked that a vehicle be sent to the end of the four-hour trail to wait for Ilat and his wife. "Roger," said the radio man. "Go get some breakfast and I'll get back to you at 8:00 to confirm your request."

Immediately after talking with the clinic, Len radioed Willis Kramer, Wycliffe's veteran radio man in Manila, asked for a consultation with a doctor, and after briefly explaining Inyap's condition, asked for urgent prayer.

In five minutes, Mary Granaas, Wycliffe's dauntless Manila housemother, had a doctor on the line. But not before she had passed Len's prayer request on to the Wycliffe members who were half way through Sunday breakfast. "Very likely," she said, "the sickness is being caused by the forces of evil. You know how Ilat has stood against the evil sacrificial system in his village."

Mary then ran into the kitchen to ask the Ifugao kitchen help to also pray. After they prayed aloud in Ifugao, Mary ran into her bedroom to pray again for healing.

Mary, at almost 70, has more energy than most people half her age and possesses an unusual amount of grace, charm, and Christian concern.

She had a deep personal interest in Ilat and the work he and Newells were doing and now she asked God to give her a verse to indicate Inyap would be healed.

Several days before in a comparative study of the Gospels, Mary noticed a medical term used by physician Luke in chapter eight, verse 44. Suddenly she was reminded of the woman Luke wrote about who had an issue of blood which was immediately *stanched* (KJV) when she touched Christ's garment. Thankfully she knelt by her bed and accepted this as one hundred percent that Inyap's blood was already *stanched*.

She was just coming into the dining room when Willis said, "You might as well stop praying for Inyap. While Len was talking to the doctor, a young Ifugao boy told Len to come immediately because Inyap was dead. Best to pray now for the family."

"I won't and can't accept that!" said Mary with her characteristic stubbornness. "God has just given me the assurance that Inyap's blood has already been *stanched*."

"Well," said Willis, "We'll have to wait twenty-four hours before Len can radio to let us know."

Two weeks later Mary, Willis, and a large group of Wycliffe workers sat in the lounge of the new Wycliffe group house and listened to Len fill in the details of the story.

After he signed off the radio, Len went back to Ilat's house with the young Ifugao boy. As they ran along the trail Len asked if Inyap was really dead. "Yes," said the young boy, "she is dead."

Len couldn't believe it was possible but as he came closer to Ilat's house he noticed a crowd of people and an old priest standing on the mountain side yelling for Inyap's spirit to come back. "Come back, come back," yelled the priest. "Don't you realize you have a newborn baby? Will you forsake your child? Don't you have pity? Don't you love your child?"

And then Len saw why everyone thought Inyap was dead. A great stream of blood lay splattered over the ground. Crushed, Ilat stood outside. Len started to talk to him and a few friends standing around when suddenly the Lord prompted him to go inside the house and look at Inyap.

He climbed the ladder and was horrified at what he found. Four women had Inyap in a semi-standing position and, according to custom, were trying to pour water down her throat (sick people always have dry throats). She was completely unconscious and if she wasn't dead from loss of blood, she soon would be from drowning. There was no visible evidence, but Len knew Inyap was not dead.

"Stop!" Len yelled. "Stop or you'll drown her! Put her down flat and elevate her legs and buttocks." Shocked at first by Len's intrusion, the women nevertheless complied.

Len backed down the stairs and went over to Ilat. "Your wife is not dead," he said gently. "Get in there and let's prepare to get her to the clinic in Banaue."

Len was sure Ilat didn't know what he was talking about but Ilat sprang up and told three other fellows to help him. Together they lifted Inyap onto the stretcher. Even then they didn't believe she was alive. "Come on," yelled Len, "we've got to get her to Banaue!"

As Ilat and the other carriers started out over the steep four-hour trail, Len ran home for a blanket and caught up with them by climbing over a steeper trail. When he caught up to them at the top of the hill, he wrapped the blanket around Inyap to keep her warm and protect her from shock. Suddenly she opened her eyes and blinked. And Len knew this was an indication from the Lord that she would live.

"But the miracle of the whole morning," said Len, "was that during the very moment you here in Manila were praying for Inyap, the Lord suddenly stopped the flow of blood. When Ilat first picked her up and laid her on the stretcher, I checked to see if there was blood coming through. There wasn't. I checked again at the top of the hill when I wrapped her in the blanket. Still no evidence of hemorrhaging. And although she remained unconscious all the way to the clinic, her issue of blood was completely *stanched* just like the woman in the Gospel of Luke!"

For a full week the believers and non-believers of Batad remained in limbo waiting for news of Inyap. If she were to die then it would confirm the pagan priest's claim that this was punishment for not following the old sacrificial system. But Inyap did not die. Miraculously she hiked back over the long hard trail she had been carried exactly one week earlier. For the first time in the experience of the young Ifugao church they saw and knew God could heal. And because they were thankful, they held a thanksgiving service to praise God for His wonderful answer to prayer.

This dramatic healing not only confounded the priests but gave renewed inspiration for the Ifugao Christians to speak out for their faith.

One of these was a new Ifugao believer who found himself an observer in a pagan sacrificial ceremony. When one of the old priests became possessed with a spirit, he picked up a live coal in his hands, flaunted his power in front of the young man and said, "See my power? I have the power of the demons."

Remembering what he had read the night before in Mark 8:33 where Christ rebuked Peter, the young man said, "You are not yourself. You are Satan! Get thee behind me, Satan!" And immediately the priest screamed in pain, dropped the coal, and rushed out.

With Inyap completely restored, Ilat and Len hiked over a 2000 foot mountain ridge to visit an area where Ilat had previously left a quantity of Scriptures. As the two men came down the other side, they suddenly heard the unmistakable strains of a gospel song Len had translated. "To hear people I had never met singing and praising the Lord in this tiny isolated mountain village was one of the greatest thrills of my twenty years in the Philippines," said Len. "Later I sat for three hours while sixty Ifugaos prayed, sang, talked about the Scriptures, and listened to Ilat build them up in their new-found faith."

Since 1970, Christian Ifugaos of Batad have conducted over sixty baptisms in the cold streams of their mountain citadel. "And," said Len, "Doreen and I constantly hear of new congregations springing up all through the Batad area. In each case they are being born from the seed of the translated Word in their own language. When people are able to read and respond to God's Word and the Holy Spirit for themselves, things really start to happen!''

# CHAPTER FOUR

## FEEDING OF THE 400

The single-engine Helio Courier approached the grassy airstrip on the broad Pulangi River in Bukidnon Province on Mindanao. It was autumn, 1970, and Wycliffe translators Ursula Post and Mary Jane Gardner peered eagerly from the plane's windows to catch sight of Bukidnon tribal friends. Ursula was returning to the Philippines from a three-month furlough in the States and Mary Jane from a brief stint at Nasuli, Wycliffe's center in the southern Philippines.

As the plane sputtered to a halt, the two women sensed something was wrong. The air of excitement customary at harvest time was missing. Instead of happy expressions, Bukidnon faces were thin and taut.

The girls soon discovered that an unknown disease had killed all their chickens, their main source of meat. Then a plague of rats swarmed over the hills, devouring everything in their path — three corn crops and the yearly rice harvest, as well as other foods on which the Bukidnon depended for survival. The predators had even eaten the roots out of the ground. Finally a flu epidemic had taken its toll of people weakened by hunger. Some had already died and others were seriously ill.

Perhaps they could help one friend — but 400! Surely the Lord who was aware of their limited support knew that clothing and feeding so many was an utter impossibility! Another Voice began to trouble the girls: "If you have a friend who is in need of food and clothing, and you say to him, 'Well, goodbye and God bless you; stay warm and eat hearty', and then don't give him clothes or food, what good does that do?" (James 2:15,16).

For seven years they had lived among the Bukidnon people in the village of Caburacanan on a 2,000-foot plateau. Although they had learned to speak the Binukid language and had begun Scripture translation, they had seen little of God's life-giving message take root in these hearts steeped in a lifetime of spirit worship. And how could two girls hope to reach more than 40,000 Bukidnon people scattered through the sawtooth mountains of the area?

What could they do? Their beloved Bukidnon were slowly starving to death. "But with God," He gently reminded them, "nothing is impossible." The girls agreed. They really should feed the village pastor and his family, they thought, and Juan Gumindo the tribal missionary who lived on the meager "support" of $20.00 a month from thirteen jungle churches. As they assumed the care of these several believers, Ursula and Mary Jane discussed with them what the Scriptures say about the believers' responsibility to care for one another as members of His body in times of need.

In a few days Anacita, their competent translation helper, called on the girls. After the usual polite greetings, she said, "Those were good words you spoke earlier from God's writings. We will see

now if your deeds are the same as your words.
What are you going to do about my family and
Tinoy's family and Luisa's family? We are all
hungry and for a long time already have not been
able to find anything to eat." So the girls extended
their commitment to cover these three families as
well.

But what about others in the village equally
hungry and weak? The girls attempted to get
government aid, but the extent of the rat plague
first had to be assessed. Even the assessors were
startled to discover more than 12,000 multiplying
rats on every two acres of land! On the basis of
their report, two organizations sent food. It lasted
a week.

Again the girls felt the burden, but how could
they possibly provide for seventy-six families? "I
was hungry and you wouldn't feed Me . . . naked,
and you wouldn't clothe Me . . . " came the insis-
tent Voice until the girls cried out in frustration.
Then suddenly God began to give the girls definite
assurance: "God will give you much so that you
can give away much . . . " Ursula and Mary Jane
yielded in obedience to God's continuing direc-
tives. They began to take definite steps to provide
for all the villagers.

The response was overwhelming. Clothing and
food came from all directions — members of the
Wycliffe "family," government agencies, people
back home, those they knew, and strangers. They
ordered regular supplies of corn grits and small
dried fish, a good source of protein. There were no
more deaths, and they could see God restoring
physical strength to the people from day to day.
The poison which the government provided

stopped the rat horde at the edge of newly-planted gardens — but it would be months before the gardens produced.

When pellagra broke out as a result of the limited diet, the doctors strongly urged switching to rice. This involved a substantial increase in price per sack of grain, and additional charges for flights to bring in the increased load. Once more Anacita challenged the hesitating missionaries. There were only 400 in their village, she reminded them, and didn't Jesus feed 5,000 with five pieces of bread and two fishes?

What a thrill to hear singing and see smiling faces again in Caburacanan! And to have God's promise, "Those you help will be glad not only because of your generous gifts to themselves and to others, but they will praise God for this proof that your deeds are as good as your doctrine" (2 Corinthians 9:13).

The relief program showed the Bukidnon that the true God cared for *them*. Instead of funerals every week, new believers were added to the body of Christ. Whereas at the beginning of the year some from thirty-two families attended the church, now most members of sixty-four of the seventy-four families turned to the Lord. Believers witnessed not only to their families in the village but to those scattered through the surrounding hills. Prayer bands visited homes of those with special needs to encourage them in the Lord. Four young people heard the Lord's call to become witnesses and enrolled in Bible school. Hunger for God's Word was so great that every bit of money the people could obtain went to buy the newly translated Scripture portions.

The testimony spread beyond Caburacanan. Juan Gumindo returned from a month's stay deep in the forests to report that the interest at the first place he visited was so great he could go no further. Although he had suffered hardship, weariness and hunger, he radiated joy — he had led twenty-four to the Lord in that place!

Recently Ursula accompanied three Bukidnon believers out to Baugo in the Dibabawon area to help Myra Lou Barnard and Jan Forster build a new house. There they found Dibabawon people hungry to know the Lord. Back again in Caburacanan, Anacita and Tinoy spurred Bukidnon believers to pray that their Dibabawon friends might soon accept Jesus. On their next trip by air to Baugo to complete the house, Juan Gumindo accompanied them, saying "God told me the harvest there is ripe."

Though uneducated, Juan spoke Dibabawon fluently enough to hold the first church service. Often during the night through thin bamboo walls Ursula heard him agonizing in prayer for various ones to whom he had witnessed. Before the week was over, ninety-three members of seventeen different families turned to the Lord, among them two elderly leaders of the area and a witch doctor. Later when Juan returned to Baugo to give new Christians further Bible teaching, he reported that seventy-three more people had turned to Christ.

The demonstration of God's love and power also transformed the spirits of the missionaries. For some time previous to her brief stateside furlough, Ursula had experienced an enervating weariness which nothing seemed to dispel. In her illness and discouragement, she had expressed to friends an urgent need for prayer. "We see little result. The Lord has used other people, but I don't see how He can use me."

Now the burden was removed and a spirit of praise replaced a spirit of heaviness. They could rest in Him and trust the future — both their own and that of the Bukidnon people — to Him.

## CHAPTER FIVE

## DON'T MAKE FACES ON MY ONION

Dick Elkins was weak with an undiagnosed illness, and with his wife Betty, they left their Manobo friends for a recuperative period in the States. It was hard for the Elkins to be away from their Manobo friends and neighbors at a time when the small Manobo church was taking its first toddler steps.

Warm and personable, Dick and Betty, in winning the hearts of the Manobos, generated a watchful and prayerful interest from their Wycliffe colleagues and supporting friends. One colleague, MariLou Weaver, out of her own interest and natural flair for writing, recorded the birth of the Bukidnon Manobo church.

" . . . In 1955 when Dick and Betty went to the village of Barandias, they built their home from hand-split mahogany boards and topped it off with a grass roof. When completed it looked like all the other houses in the village and in this setting of neighborly identification, Dick and Betty learned the

Manobo language while simultaneously ministering to the needs of the Manobo community.

One of the first people to understand why the Elkins came to live in his community was Siblian, Dick's language teacher.

"Good friend," said Siblian to Dick one day as he worked in his garden, "what is the medicine for a person whose thinking leaves him?"

"There are many kinds of medicine," said Dick. "But sometimes a person needs more than medicine. Who is sick like this?"

"It is Anuy," said Siblian. "He is like a wild animal. This morning he went to the burial place and dug up a grave and pulled out the body of Mampiyanu's girl who died a short time ago."

"Do you remember the story about the demoniac of the Gadarenes we translated this morning?" said Dick.

"Ah," said Siblian thoughtfully, "Anuy must have an evil spirit. But what can we do?"

"The only thing we can do," said Dick. "Pray."

"But," asked Siblian, "how do we pray?"

"We talk to God as if we're talking to our best friend," said Dick. "Betty and I will ask God to drive out the evil spirit. And you pray, too."

When they went into the house several
women began talking with Betty in
excited, frightened voices about Anuy's
plight. Their fear was spine chillingly
dark and gloomy. With Siblian looking
on in silence, Dick and Betty committed
Anuy to the Lord for His protection.

Early the next morning Dick and
Betty left Barandias for Nasuli. When
they returned a month later, Dick
immediately asked about Anuy.

"He is well, completely well," said
Siblian. "The evil spirit left him the day
you left." Then in a voice that reflected
his amazement said, "Your praying is
really strong!"

MariLou continued her report with the effect
this had on Siblian.

" . . . Two years later Siblian and two
other Manobo men surrendered their
lives to Christ. With a limited supply of
translated Scripture portions, Dick and
Betty hastily instructed the new believers in basic Christian truths before
they left for a year's furlough.

When Dick and Betty returned they
found the three believers had increased
to seven and all were meeting for Bible
study in Siblian's home."

But before Dick began to translate the Scriptures, he learned to exercise unusual sensitivity
toward Manobo culture and customs. He and Betty

discovered they must never talk to a dog, laugh at a cow, sell a cat, marry a first cousin, or make fun of a caterpillar. But they didn't know it was wrong to make faces on an onion.

It was their daughter Kathleen's birthday and she received a potato head kit complete with tiny eyes, noses, mustaches, and eye glasses. Lacking a potato, Kathleen dressed up two onions and created what to her and the family were two comical figures.

The Manobos, however, failed to see the humor. When Kathleen's younger brother playfully showed the 'onion faces' to two Manobo girls, their frightened screams caused Dick to seek an explanation. When he learned of the taboo he quickly apologized to the village elders.

Dick and Betty were not afraid of the punishment of lightning, thunder, and hail the Manobos believed would come because they had broken the taboo. Rather they wanted the Manobos to know they apologized because they respected their customs. Months later when a few had believed, Dick taught the story of Christ calming the storm which in turn opened up a meaningful discussion of how Christ, not an evil spirit, controls the elements.

The development of the Manobo church was full of surprises, too. In eleven years it grew to forty-five including Anuy and Mampiyano and almost from the beginning, patterns developed which Dick and Betty would never have predicted.

Dick, a keen Bible translator and cultural anthropologist, understood his mission was to *introduce* the Gospel, not *shape* it. And because he believed that the church should not be built around an individual, Dick carefully allowed the form of the Manobo church to be shaped out of their own cultural patterns and language.

As each new Manobo accepted the Gospel, he began reaching out to his immediate family and nearest relatives. And when they were reached they in turn assumed responsibility for their family and relatives.

For nine years Siblian lead the small group of believers as lay pastor. But as the church grew, other leaders were chosen according to Manobo cultural patterns which demanded an older more respected man who had the right to teach and rebuke.

Another form that came into shape was the announcement spot during the Manobo church service. One Sunday a visiting lowland pastor told the Manobo brethren their service was "incorrect" because they didn't allow for this important segment in their service. After consulting Dick (who said it was up to them), the Manobo brethren decided to incorporate this as part of their regular service.

The following Sunday a Manobo leader announced that between the Sunday School class and preaching service they would have announcement time. Puzzled, Dick waited for the appropriate moment. When it came he was dumfounded. The Manobos had interpreted announcements to mean a time when they would publicly confess any ill feelings they had for one another, *announce* how the Lord had blessed them, or if they had sinned, ask forgiveness not only from the Lord but from any they might have offended!

As the church grew, Dick pushed ahead on translation while Betty spent many long, hard hours hiking over steep difficult trails each week teaching people to read and write. "We sense a new feeling of self respect rather than inferiority when they carry a Manobo book under their arm," Betty wrote.

Then in 1971 Dick suddenly became ill and he and Betty returned to the States. And during their eighteen month absence, the Manobo church doubled its membership. "Due in part," said Associate Director Chuck Walton, "to the Elkins' strong literacy and translation program. And because of their love for the people and wisdom in keeping a hands off policy, the church came to see its own community responsibility."

Part of this responsibility was to assume the partial support of a Filipino missionary. After hearing about this young man who was on his way to New Guinea, the Manobo church voted to give him ten pesos ($1.43) each *month*. Their previous giving for an entire *year* was $5.00! In their enthusiasm for this new ministry, the church voted to take on the support of two other missionaries for the same amount. Their missionary giving eventually equalled the yearly income of two Manobo families. Not only did the young Manobo church keep their commitments, they ended their first year of giving with $83.00 in the treasury (of which most was given to Filipino missionaries).

In April 1972 during the middle of their sick leave, Betty wrote: "Two weeks ago we discovered the cause of Dick's illness that brought us home last year. It was diagnosed as hypoglycemia (low blood sugar) .... The Manobo church continues to grow and they write of their need for a larger chapel. Our hearts were warmed to learn that fifty-five new literates graduated from the first series of classes taught by Manobo teachers who were trained last spring by our co-workers, George and Valerie Hires. We expect this literacy evangelism ministry to expand into the southern half of the province next year." (As 1973 began there were 300 Manobos who had learned to read and write in literacy programs supervised by the Hires.)

Nine months later back in the Philippines, Dick and Betty wrote: "As we look to the future Betty and I expect to finish our work among the Manobos within five years. This means the completion of the New Testament and portions of the Old. It will also mean an indigenous, growing, reproducing, literate church. In addition there will be a number of Manobo authors producing Christian literature to ensure that literacy remains a positive value in Manobo culture."

The letter further described their plans for Scripture and hymn translation, a cassette tape ministry, reading classes, and colportage work in order to distribute more widely the available Scripture portions.

That the Manobo church is growing is obvious and, Lord willing, the Elkins will leave, as did Paul when he had unfolded God's secret plan.

In presenting this cross section of Wycliffe work in the Philippines one is tempted to ask, "Why hasn't God worked the same in each case?"

Director Morris Cottle may help with the answer.

" . . . One of the lessons I am learning is that God has not sent us into the world to plot the course of the church; to decide who and when it should be born . . . The area where God seems to be doing the most is where people have taken a deep interest in the translated Scriptures and where our translators have refused to become involved in the organizational shaping and structuring of a local church."

For all their natural skill and freedom to create, too many ethnic minorities do not yet enjoy the free gift of spiritual liberty.

PART TWO

**THE JOY OF A LOVING JONATHAN**

# PREFACE

The first section of this book focused on the church, barriers to spiritual progress, and difficulties translators frequently experience when facing a culture different than their own. My desire in Part One was for you to know better how to pray and understand your counterpart in his hand-to-hand ministry of touching people and sharing with them God's great secret.

My attempt now is to expose our humanity so that when you meet us you will accept us as brother and sisters with a common creatureliness. Because we know, as do you, the most effective learning and character maturing comes from the Body of Christ and a clear understanding of our interdependence.

# CHAPTER ONE

## THE JOY OF A LOVING JONATHAN

One of the geniuses of William Shakespeare was his ability to introduce a wide variety of different characters. And no matter how small the role, each became significant to the entire epic.

Beginning October 17, 1971 — a Sunday evening — God, in a small Vietnamese community, brought together a divergent cast to create a story more poignant, beautiful, and triumphal than, in my opinion, the greatest of Shakespearean dramas. The principles are Marilyn and Ken Smith, their two-year-old son Jonathan, two Wycliffe school teachers — Janie Voss and Karen Gunnette — and a young GI named Ed.

Because this is really Marilyn's story and those who lived it, I want them to tell it. I'll help by editing, linking, and introducing some of the cast (many unnamed) as each instinctively, out of Christian love, wept with those who wept. As in no other writing experience, I met developing people who for a moment in time were fully conscious of their humanity.

After their official assignment to Vietnam, Ken and Marilyn arrived in Saigon on May 5, 1962, four months later than originally planned. Reason —

their first child, Linda, decided to make her appearance two months ahead of schedule!

In August, after almost three months of Vietnamese language study, the Smiths moved out of their cement house in the lowlands to a mud and bamboo house in the central highlands town of Kontum. Though small, Kontum is heavily populated with representatives of a dozen ethnic minority groups. One of these is the Sedang for whom the Smiths felt burdened to begin a program of Bible translation.

Because the Smiths are, according to Director Dick Pittman, "systematic, organized, and disciplined," they made rapid progress in their study of Vietnamese. By January 1963 they divided their time between Vietnamese and the Sedang language.

However, the Smiths knew the best way to learn a new language was to immerse themselves in its environment. And in July they moved from Kontum to the district center in Dakto, a highland town surrounded by Sedang villages. Almost immediately they had daily contact with Sedang children who came to leaf through their picture books. And when the children told their parents there was nothing to fear, their mothers came selling bean sprouts, bamboo shoots, and bananas. Not to be outdone, the fathers came with such important items as live parrots and snakes (the boa make delicious eating!).

While it wasn't possible to secure constant language help, the Smiths did make progress. "Their monthly work reports," said Dick Pittman, "always gave a realistic appraisal of their situation and were marked with a sparkle of faith and hope."

Ken and Marilyn Smith live their life in Viet Nam realisti-
cally and with "a sparkle of faith and hope." (Ken pictured
on following page.)

By February 1964, after the birth of Smith's first son David, the tiny resolute Vietnam branch (about 35 members) struggled to keep abreast of the heavy translation load coming in from other teams. Building on the experience of Wycliffe's Mexico branch, they began to establish a workshop center where translators could come and receive individual help and evaluation from experienced translators.

Because most of South Vietnam's ethnic minorities are located in the central highlands, Kontum seemed an ideal spot for the center. And because Ken was not only resident in the area but held an engineering degree, he seemed the ideal person to help oversee the workshop construction.

By the end of 1964, linguistic, translation, and literacy facilities were set up and operating in handsome white-washed buildings made from thousands of pressed mud bricks. After the construction oversight, Ken and Marilyn continued their work in the Sedang language and before leaving for furlough in the Spring of 1967, completed a translation of the life of Christ and Luke 15. They were to return the following spring, but the infamous 1968 Tet offensive arrived first.

When it was over, the recently built Kontum workshop lay in ruins.* With Ken's translated Scriptures and primers lost in the destruction and security in Kontum uncertain, the Smiths were asked to serve a year in the Philippines as house

---

* A full account of what happened to Kontum, Wycliffe personnel, other missionaries and Christian workers, is covered in James C. Hefley's book, *By Life or By Death*, Zondervan, 1972.

Ken Smith

parents in the Nasuli children's home. (Because many of the first Wycliffites to enter Vietnam in 1958 were Philippine branch workers who transferred to Vietnam, the two branches enjoy a special bond of love and cooperation. The children's home and school in Nasuli is one of their cooperative ventures.)

After fulfilling this assignment with their usual competence and willingness, the Smiths returned to Vietnam in November 1969. And while becoming reacquainted with their colleagues, happily introduced a new son — Jonathan.

In June 1970 the Smiths were assigned to the newly acquired workshop site in Nha Trang, 250 miles north of Saigon. Ken, who now held the position of Deputy Director for Nha Trang, eagerly dug into a program of preparing Sedang text books and helping other members with their literacy and translation materials.

By the time "Jonny" reached his second birthday, his bright personality made him the unofficial mascot of the Vietnamese branch. Older children, Vietnamese nationals, single girls, and moms and dads who knew him, loved him for his fun-loving giggle and half-stumbling run when they chased him. And when they caught him, he almost always got the hiccups from his effervescent laughter.

In October 1971, after a Branch conference in January and several workshops, the Smiths and other families began to feel the tension of long hours, high humidity, and the uncertainty of war. Trained to live in crowded, cramped conditions, most Wycliffites take group living as a matter of course. "But," said Marilyn, "the over-crowded common dining room and two bathrooms to serve

Wycliffe school children in Viet Nam have the South China Sea as their swimming pool.

thirty people were getting to me. In fact, I couldn't step out of my room to go anywhere without having to smile at people I didn't feel like smiling at! All of us were engaged in Christian work and loved the Lord, but frictions mounted. We became indifferent and sometimes cold to one another."

During this time, Gini Steinkamp, a Christian and Missionary Alliance missionary, along with a number of other women missionaries, began a Monday evening sharing and prayer time. Marilyn, because she was hungry for fellowship and Bible study, began attending. On her second visit she shared her feelings of discouragement and Gini prayed for her.

"I was touched when Gini asked God to reach into every room and touch each person at the group house before the workshop ended in two weeks," said Marilyn. And after that meeting, Marilyn repeated the same prayer several times during the week and wondered how God would answer.

In the meantime, the breakdown in interpersonal relationships was too big a word for Jonny to worry about. His days were filled with warmth, happiness, and people who loved him.

One of those who loved him very much was Janie Voss, a tall, attractive, dark-haired school teacher who came to Vietnam in 1970 from the Philippine branch to begin a school in Nha Trang. The site chosen for the primary school and the children's home was a chunk of waterfront property set in a snug cove on the South China Sea, far removed from the war zone.

Few American children have a more idyllic school ground. Tall royal palms sway in breezes

Primary school teaching for Karen Gunnette and Janie Voss is more than just a job. Both are grateful to God for meaningful work.

that seem to beg all self-respecting Vietnamese boys to shimmy up the slender trunks and kick loose the clusters of bowling ball-size coconuts. And when they oblige, the school children return to classes laughing, chewing on a plug of white coconut meat.

There are monkey bars and soft white sand for those who slip and fall. Balmy afternoons to swim in the rich blue sea and snorkle in kelp beds. And for those who don't swim, there are rocks to climb and a crescent-shaped mile-long white sand beach to explore.

It was on this beach each morning that Janie, dressed in crisp cotton prints, greeted outgoing fishermen on her way to school.

At first the new school and stunning natural beauty of her half-mile stroll made Janie's life unbelievably calm and uncomplicated. She was grateful to God for meaningful work and her new staff teacher and friend, Karen Gunnette. At twenty-six Karen was vivacious, well-traveled, sensitive, and a perfect compliment to Janie's reserved personality. Like Janie, Karen's teaching was more than just a job. She loved the children and they loved her.

But then in August, Janie began to think seriously about giving it all up.

# CHAPTER TWO

## FRIENDS AND ANGELS ARE THE SAME

Like Marilyn, Janie and Karen felt the disquieting effects of petty problems germinating in a hotbed of frustration at the Nha Trang workshop. "The problems," said Karen, "were mostly crummy little things. Like people getting upset because someone misplaced the keys or forgot to put gas in the group VW bus. Or after having signed up for the bus finding it gone when you went for it. Others were frustrated because the children distracted them from their work with their noise." And because Karen knew prayer was the only way to change the brewing discontent, she met with a small group of friends to ask God to soothe the abrasive frictions.

Meanwhile, Janie, who identified with Karen and her concern over the growing tension, struggled with a different problem. She had an expanding feeling of self-doubt and conflict between what she knew she was and wanted to be, and what she felt her constituency demanded her "missionary image" should be.

"For as long as I can remember," said Janie, "my ambition was to be a teacher on a mission field. And as soon as I realized I had a talent for this, I aimed to reach this goal."

That ambition was realized in the fall of 1968 after Bible school, college, travel to Europe, two years of practical teaching, and S.I.L. training. Janie was first assigned to teach the children of Wycliffe parents taking their Jungle Camp training in southern Mexico. Following this she taught for a year in the Philippines before her final assignment in Vietnam.

Yet with her proven ability and obvious devotion to a work she considered deeply important, Janie wanted to resign. "Mostly," she said, "because I couldn't and wasn't being a real and honest person to myself, my church, and friends at home, and because I felt like a hypocrite when I repeatedly found myself depressed and unhappy in the service of the Lord. I also knew the children's lives would be affected if I didn't have the joy of the Lord."

In mid-October, Janie felt her spiritual condition desperate enough to plead with God to take any measure He wanted in her life. "Lord, I don't care what it takes," she prayed one day as she walked along the beach, "but please give me a sense of Your presence. Only don't touch the children."

Three days later God answered.

"I think we should both go to the dedication of our new headquarters site in Saigon," said Ken to Marilyn.

"I do, too," said Marilyn. "David and Linda are in school, but what about Jonny? I don't like leaving him but it will be difficult to care for him and attend meetings."

Ken thought the change and rest would do them good. "Let's pray about it," he said, "and see what happens."

Janie Voss greated outgoing fishermen each morning on her way to teach school.

Three days later on Saturday morning, Marilyn, in casual conversation with Janie, told her she was still unsure about taking Jonny to the dedication service. "Why, I'd be happy to look after him for a couple of days," said Janie. Then with a warm smile that showed her two big dimples said, "You know he and I have something going. He's so precious!"

Air America's C-46 afternoon flight to Saigon on Sunday, October 17, 1971, was for Marilyn and Ken easy, comfortable, and relaxing. At first Marilyn found it strange to be without Jonny. "I've never left him with anyone before," she confided later to a friend at Saigon's International Protestant Church. And although she expressed perfect confidence in Janie, she found it difficult not to wonder how he was behaving and what he was doing. But after the 7:00 church service, the Smiths were caught up in a splendid wave of warm Christian fellowship with their Wycliffe colleagues and momentarily enjoyed the full consciousness of the eternal present.

Part of this warmth was generated by two highly personable friends, Ralph and Lorraine Haupers, who invited the Smiths, Jackie Maier, Eva Burton (Wycliffe translators), and an Air Force major to their apartment for refreshments.

When they arrived at the Hauper apartment they found a movie company running noisy generators outside their front door. "Come on in," said Lorraine cheerily. "We have a third-floor back porch that will block out all that noise."

This simple move was shortly to prove providential, because in Nha Trang, God's foreordained plan for Jonny was about to begin.

Linda Bryant, a Wycliffe guest helper and her Air Force husband Bob, were a few minutes late for the Nha Trang English chapel service at Camp McDermott. When they entered the chapel, Jonny, who was standing up on the pew between Janie and Karen, immediately spotted them and gave them his biggest "Hi!"

"We smiled," said Linda, "and noticed how he followed us across the room with his alert inquisitive eyes." Linda smiled again as she saw Jonny sticking his toy helicopter into Karen's shoulder-length hair. Later, after the manner of most two-year-olds who miss their afternoon nap, Jonny gave Karen and Janie a few moments reprieve by falling asleep. Then just before the service ended, Linda noticed Janie get up and leave. Karen followed with Jonny in her arms.

By previous arrangement Karen had agreed to go with Janie only if she could leave the chapel in time to meet with three other Wycliffe women at the Center who wanted to pray again for the strained relationships.

Half of the ten-minute drive from the chapel to the center was through heavy traffic. But Janie, accustomed to the capricious driving habits of the Vietnamese, carefully guided her borrowed two-door right-hand drive VW sedan along the highway. The evening was warm and Karen wound down her side window for Jonny.

Suddenly something caught the corner of her eye. Karen looked up. Two yellow headlights appeared on a collision course directly in front of her. Then she heard it. The heavy horrible slam of metal smashing against metal. Her only words were

"Oh no!" before the splintering glass became for her a million lovely stars, and all was silent.

Back at the chapel, Linda and Bob stood with the other worshippers to sing the closing hymn. Halfway through, the phone rang. Chaplain Davis was called out and in a few moments returned and asked an associate to close in prayer.

When the meeting ended, Linda began reminiscing with a friend who sat next to her about all the good things the Lord had taught and done for them during their time in Vietnam. Chaplain Davis walked over to join them, his face serious.

"I wonder," he said, "if you ladies would come over to the dispensary with me. Janie and Karen have been in an accident."

Immediately Linda's memory of Jonny standing in the pew flashed across her mind. "What about Jonny?" she asked.

"He was killed," said Chaplain Davis. "He died instantly from an impact on the back of his head. The girls will need your comfort."

The almost head-on crash caused Janie's VW and what turned out to be a U.S. Army pickup, to spin around and slide into ditches on opposite sides of the road. Miraculously, no passersby were hurt.

"When the car finally thudded to a stop in the ditch," said Janie, "I felt the immediate *presence* of the Lord. It was beyond anything I had ever experienced. Even when I saw Karen and Jonny and thought both were dead, God's extraordinary presence and direction enabled me to say, 'Thank You, Lord. Praise the Lord.' " (This new sense of the Lord's presence was so evident that Ken later said, "From that moment Janie has been a transformed person." Linda Bryant said, "Subsequent days revealed depths in Janie's person that hadn't been apparent to me before.")

Both Janie and Karen said the accident happened so fast it was difficult to remember what happened. "I was in a slight shock when I came to," said Karen. "I looked down and was astounded to see Jonny in my arms. I couldn't figure out why he should be with me or why I was holding him. What was left of my door, was open and before I climbed out, Janie reached over and took Jonny from me.

"As I stood by the crumpled car and prayed with Janie for God to help us, I remember being unusually calm in spite of a large crowd of excited Vietnamese who were beginning to gather. Both of us seemed fine except for a cut on Janie's knee. I was beginning to feel my several bruises and my leg was bleeding from a broken blood vessel."

But now their concern was for Jonny. Inside, both knew he was with the Lord but didn't want to admit it. Then Janie thought about Marilyn and Ken. Jonny had been her responsibility and she wondered how she would be able to tell them their baby was dead.

At that moment an unidentified American off-duty M.P. pushed his way out of the crowd toward the wreckage and offered his help. Quickly and expertly he sped the two teachers and the little body back to Camp McDermott and the American emergency clinic.

Ed, the driver of the wrecked Army pickup, smelled of liquor and was taken into custody by the U.S. Army M.P.'s. A subsequent blood test revealed he was far beyond the legal limit for liquor consumption while driving. It was also discovered that Ed was driving the pickup without authorization.

A Vietnamese national who witnessed the accident rushed to the Wycliffe workshop center and told the news to Vurnell and Max Cobbey. (Vurnell lost her first husband eight years earlier in a Viet Cong road-block ambush.) Still another phoned Chaplain Davis.

As Linda drove to the dispensary with Chaplain Davis she thought about little Jonny and how cute and lovable he had been during the service and how much Ken and Marilyn would need the Lord's comfort. She also wondered how or what she could say or do that would be helpful at such a time. "But," said Linda, "when I walked into the emergency room and saw Karen, I felt a deep desire to just go over and be with her without words."

Karen's first words to Linda were, "I'm all right. Janie's in the next room with Jonny. Go to her." At that moment Janie walked in. They encouraged her to lay down on a physician's table but she made repeated attempts to sit up because she wanted to thank the man who brought them from the accident to the dispensary. She also expressed her concern for the young GI who had hit them. "Pray for him," she said.

Within twenty minutes after the accident, the dispensary was filled with Wycliffe colleagues, friends from other missions, and people who barely knew them.

"When the missionaries began arriving at the dispensary," said Janie, "I thought I was seeing angels! Wycliffe folks, C&MA and Baptist folks all came — friends and angels *are* the same! In that instant the Lord taught me how much we need each other and challenged me to be honestly concerned for people. I prayed and asked the Lord to forgive my past neglect of others."

Linda Bryant was impressed how each person was needed and thought of some personal way to help. Betty Banker soaked Janie's bloodstained dress to remove that reminder; the Cobbey's thought of removing Jonny's playthings from Janie's home before she returned; and others made arrangements for Janie and Karen to spend the night at the workshop center.

After a medic placed three stitches in Janie's knee, both girls and their friends left. All except Jim Cooper. He tried to reach Ken and Marilyn in Saigon by phone. As he repeatedly tried to make connection, Janie's words of testimony kept coming into his mind: "I had the assurance that I was not in the wrong and could not have prevented it. When I tried to feel guilty the Lord took it away and seemed to say, 'Ken and Marilyn are prepared' and then He covered me with His peace."

Later in their upstairs room, Bob Bryant read to Linda from Spurgeon's *Morning and Evening:* "He shall gather the lambs with his arms (Isaiah 40:11)," and then Bob tenderly held Linda in his arms.

# CHAPTER THREE

## HE LIVES

After ten years in Vietnam as a literacy expert, perky and warm hearted Eugenia Johnston has experienced more than her share of war and turmoil. She was evacuated under heavy fire from Kontum during TET of 1968 only to spend two more harrowing nights in sandbag bunkers of a beseiged U.S. Army compound. "But," confessed Eugenia, "nothing I ever experienced in the war zone was as difficult as being asked to notify the Smiths of Jonny's death."

Two hours after the accident, Jim Cooper finally got through to Wycliffe's tiny Saigon business office. Eugenia, who had an upstairs office-living apartment, answered Jim's late Sunday evening call. Eugenia, a deeply kind and sensitive person, could not bring herself to face the Smiths with such devastating news. Rather, she decided the most accessible elected branch administrative officer should notify them. That person was Ralph Haupers. Believing the Smiths to be at the new headquarters, Eugenia drove to the Hauper apartment and rang the door bell. It was 10:30 p.m.

Wondering who the late caller was, Lorraine ran down the three flights of stairs and opened the front door. Had the Smiths been sitting in the living room they would have been in plain view. But all they heard from the upstairs porch was Lorraine's warm, half-surprised, "Well, hello!" Then dead silence.

At first Marilyn only slightly wondered about the silence. Lorraine then called Ralph, and in a few minutes, Ken. "By this time," said Marilyn, "I was getting nervous but never once thought whatever was happening would involve me. It just seemed strange that everyone was downstairs and I couldn't hear them talking."

"When Ralph called me down," said Ken later, "he and Lorraine led me into the front bedroom and had me sit on the bed. No words before or since have been more staggering or paralyzing. Yet immediately after Ralph told me I somehow knew this was in God's plan."

Ralph then called Marilyn into the bedroom. "Our Jonny has been killed in an accident," said Ken, gripping Marilyn's delicate shoulders in his strong hands. "The two teachers were with him."

Then in a spontaneous response that came from his living faith, Ken began to quote Job 1:21. But as he started to repeat, "The Lord gave and the Lord has . . . ," Marilyn later admitted she didn't want him to go on. "At that moment I hated that verse," she said. "I didn't want my little Jonny to be taken away. I wanted him back and I wanted to shut the words out from my ears." But Ken finished, " . . . the Lord has taken away, blessed be the name of the Lord."

As Ken and Marilyn fell on their knees beside the bed, Ralph and Lorraine turned and left them alone to weep and pray. For many minutes Marilyn and Ken prayed for the Lord's strength and asked His help to accept this as from Him.

"After we poured out our hearts," said Ken, "we knew there were many things to do and got up from our knees. As we did, Marilyn thought of the words to a song: *I sing for I cannot be silent. My Father planned it all.* We embraced and went out to meet our friends."

Through the courtesy of Hauper's military guest Major Chuck Thompson, all were invited to the MACV Headquarters at Saigon Airbase. Here they were whisked through security guards and Ken, with the efficient Air Force communication system at his disposal, spent several hours phoning.

His first call was to Jim Cooper in Nha Trang. Ken and Marilyn wanted to find out more details and specifically reassure Janie and Karen of their love. "Please tell Janie," said Ken, "that we entrusted Jonny to her with our love and confidence. And despite the events, hold no resentment. We love her and Karen very much."

"Ken's words greatly helped to encourage us," said Janie later, "though never for a moment did we question the Smith's love."

As Ken and Marilyn waited for the operator to make connections with their pastor in New Jersey, Ralph encouraged them. "You know," he said, "Pastor Bubna preached on the goodness of God this morning. He quoted from Joseph Bayly's booklet *When a Child Dies*. The pastor said that after losing three sons from an incurable disease, Bayly said, 'I have learned that God is sovereign and in times of great stress, *reason* is a deceptively weak crutch for *faith*. Because REASON GROPES

IN THE DARK FOR ANSWERS, WHILE FAITH WAITS FOR GOD.' "

Much later Marilyn said it was this timely word from Ralph which enabled her to begin the difficult adjustment of accepting Jonny's death. Because while Marilyn knew she must come to grips with this heart-ripping event, she began to flagellate herself with thoughts about whether she had been right in leaving Jonny. "But each time I began to think like that," said Marilyn, "Joe Bayly's words returned to comfort me."

With no available flights back to Nha Trang that evening, Ken and Marilyn waited out the night at the new headquarters. "Our tears came easy," said Ken, "as we spent a deeply precious time far into the early morning talking to each other and to the Lord. Finally we realized we had to catch a 7:15 a.m. flight and would need physical strength to meet the many demands in Nha Trang. We asked the Lord for a little sleep and He granted it. Our hearts were at rest."

On Monday morning, October 18, when Linda Bryant walked into the Wycliffe office in Nha Trang, she found a Vietnamese secretary weeping uncontrollably. "I just found out," she sobbed. "What can I do?" Remembering her first sense of frustration the night before, Linda felt hesitant to offer a simplistic word of advice. "I don't know what it is that will meet your heart's need," she said tenderly, "because each of us have different needs. The Lord is the *only* One who can do that something special in our hearts at a time like this." Then remembering Ken had expressed keen concern and hope that all special workshop assignments be completed on schedule, said, "I suggest we do our best to complete all our assignments as Ken asked us to do."

After arriving back in Nha Trang aboard the same C-46 that took them relaxed and happy to Saigon, the Smiths were met and embraced by more than a dozen friends and colleagues. A number of those who met them were people who did not personally share Ken and Marilyn's faith in Jesus Christ and who admitted their own hopelessness in the face of death. With quiet dignity, warmth, and enthusiasm, Ken briefly shared his faith, pointing out the only way to dissolve their hopelessness about eternity was for them individually to be intimately acquainted with God as seen in Jesus Christ. "It's because we have and continue to respond personally to Jesus Christ and what He tells us in His Word — the Bible — that we believe all things are planned by Him. And because of this we believe and accept Jonny's death as part of that plan."

For some Ken's words held no personal meaning or identification. Yet as Ken and Marilyn lived those words in the hard crunch of everyday life experience, some Vietnamese and Americans suddenly understood for the first time what Christian love was all about.

Onlookers at the airport noticed Marilyn's willingness to accept God's plan and were impressed with the strength she had to comfort a woman who only twenty minutes earlier had heard the news. The woman vicariously placed herself in Marilyn's position and was troubled as she wondered how she would accept the loss of her own small child.

Others heard Ken's request to see Janie and Karen before their own two children Linda and David. (They had been told of their brother's death by house parents John and Carolyn Miller.) "We knew the girls had born the heaviest burden of the ordeal," said Ken, "and wanted to personally comfort and reassure them."

Later at the Wycliffe house after funeral arrangements were made, Wycliffites in turn came to see the Smiths. "This was most amazing to me," said Marilyn. "Because for the first time in years all our petty problems and misunderstandings were gone. There was nothing but sympathy and love. Often someone came to give us a hug or place a strong silent arm around our shoulder."

Some came to ask forgiveness for past misunderstandings. Others who felt they should have volunteered to take Jonny for the weekend needed the Smiths' reassurance that this was in God's plan. "After all," said Marilyn, "God could have stopped the accident just as easily as He allowed it."

"I know," said one woman pensively, "but Jonny belonged to everyone. It was as if he were our own little boy and now each of us suffers together." (For weeks later a much heard prayer was, "God, don't let us forget what it cost to make us love each other.")

As the woman spoke, Marilyn was reminded of her friend's earlier prayer for God to touch each person in every room and to bring them together in love. God indeed had not only reached into every room in the Nha Trang workshop, but like ripples from a stone thrown into a clear pool of deep water, was reaching out beyond the tiny confines of the Wycliffe family.

The first of these ripples touched almost a hundred people at the three o'clock funeral and memorial service where Wycliffe workers, American servicemen (some from the softball team where Jonny had chased after stray balls), Vietnamese nationals, ethnic minorities, and outside missionary friends listened to Chaplain Davis. Under a hot glistening sun, Chaplain Davis smiled and beckoned the crowd closer to the graveside. "We've come together this afternoon to praise the Lord," he began. Then acting on Ken's suggestion, gave a message simple enough for each child to understand the meaning of death and the Christian hope of resurrection.

"Your little friend and brother is now in heaven with Jesus Christ. He is there because our bodies are not like the crabs we see along the beach. When a crab's body is destroyed, that's the end. There is nothing more. But Jesus Christ said that even though our bodies might be destroyed, the real you inside lives on forever. And when Jonny's body died yesterday, he immediately went to heaven and is there now with the Lord Jesus Christ. And he is far happier and far better off than he would be on earth . . . "

The chaplain's words, though simple, were enough to enlighten and help many of the children who viewed Jonny's death with perplexity and deep sadness. This emphasis helped Jonny's sister Linda to change her prayer from, "Lord help us not to miss Jonny," to, "Thank you, Jesus, for taking Jonny to heaven."

When the service ended, Ken and Marilyn stood with their arms around Janie and Karen in a "circle of love." Beside them was a small rounded dirt mound with a cross of white gladiolas made by a Chru tribesman. Pinned to the cross on a satin streamer were the words, "He lives." Later, someone gave them the words of Samuel Rutherford: "You have not lost a child. Nay not lost to you who is found in Christ. *He is not sent away but only sent before.*"

# CHAPTER FOUR

## VICTORY!

Although the Apostle John recorded Christ's words in clear unambiguous language in his first Epistle, not all believers have sufficient strength to obey the command to "love one another." Man, because he is man (his Christianity notwithstanding), frequently requires sharp reminders that his life is not his own. God's desire is that His children's lives be progressively more and more like Jesus. Many of those close to the events at the beginning and during the days and weeks following Jonny's death experienced a fresh expectancy and surprising evidence of spiritual growth in their pilgrimage to be conformed to the image of His Son.

Several days later during a readjustment time at a C&MA vacation cottage, the Smiths wrote: " . . . In every detail of life we are sensing the real awe of what God is beginning to do among us."

Some of the first evidences were letters which met Ken and Marilyn in their special need. One such letter written before the accident came from a Mr. Stearns who with his wife had showered special grandparent-like love upon the Smiths and their children. "I am enclosing a check for $15.00," he wrote. "This past year Grandma Stearns died and I didn't feel I knew how or what to buy the children for Christmas. Instead I have sent this check for the three children."

When Marilyn told Linda and David they each had five dollars to spend for Christmas, both immediately dug out the catalogs and began looking through the pages for their gifts. But Ken and Marilyn wondered what to do with Jonny's money. Finally after some discussion and prayer Ken wrote Grampa Stearns of their decision. "Because Jonny's death occurred while we were in Saigon to thank the Lord for our new headquarters site, we have decided to use Jonny's portion to start a Jonny Memorial Fund to help provide a single women's apartment complex in the new headquarters building. He was so loved by the single girls we think this will be appropriate."

From the same vacation cottage Ken also wrote: "We have never asked 'why?'. Yet the answers seem to come to us through the lives we have been able to touch."

One of those the Smiths touched was a high ranking presidential advisor who came to offer his condolences. "At first," said Marilyn, "we didn't know who he was or how important a position he held in the military. He came with a USAID liason man whom we knew and we just started talking and sharing what we believed to be God's plan for Jonny and our own hope of eternal life. Then as we assured him of our love and concern for Ed, our military guest suddenly, with eyes brimming, excused himself and left."

Ken and Marilyn later discovered the advisor was overwhelmed with the Smiths' attitude of loving forgiveness.

Equally amazed was the Vietnamese civilian community. Many, including a Vietnamese pastor, felt it culturally abnormal for the Smiths not to express hatred for Ed and want revenge. "This was the first time," said Dick Pittman, "that many understood the meaning of loving one's enemies and doing good to those who hurt you."

While Marilyn never wanted revenge, she said at first it didn't matter to her if she ever met Ed. However, Ken felt healing would come faster to all if they could meet and talk together with Ed as friends. Through Chaplain Davis he arranged a meeting on the 21st.

"I remember looking out the window waiting for Chaplain Davis to drive up," said Marilyn. "They were a little late and my mind was filled with, 'Why do I have to meet him? I have forgiven him. It doesn't matter now if I meet him. I really don't care.' "

When Chaplain Davis finally drove into the driveway, Marilyn and Ken noticed that Ed didn't get out to open the gate. He sat there dejectedly with his head slumped on his chest. They invited them in and Ken extended his hand and told Ed they were glad he came. But all the twenty-three-year-old GI could do was sink into the couch and weep uncontrollably.

After seeing how young and completely broken Ed was, Marilyn's heart melted. "At that moment," she said, "I cared. And I've cared ever since!"

Realizing coherent conversation was impossible, the Smiths turned to Chaplain Davis and related how God was working through the circumstances of the past few days. After almost thirty minutes

Ed finally composed himself enough to talk briefly with the Smiths.

Quietly, and still broken, Ed told of letters he had written to his parents telling of the accident. Although he did not know Jesus Christ personally, he acknowledged that God was somehow in the events of the past days.

After Ken read 1 Thessalonians 4:13, he gave Ed a New Testament and the book *Prison to Praise*.* Marilyn then explained how two — Christ and Jonny — had died to bring him to God and further explained the reason for the life and death of Jesus Christ.

"That's just what Chaplain Davis told me," said Ed through his tears. As they talked, all wept together. With arms of love around his shoulder, the Smiths walked Ed back to the jeep and drove with him and the Chaplain to visit the two teachers.

As they drove the Smiths learned that Ed, a former school teacher, had taught grades seven to nine. They also learned he had extended his time in Vietnam for an additional six months to cut down his total military obligation.

After greeting Janie and Karen (they had briefly met Ed before at the army dispensary), the chaplain suggested they all pray. "And what a prayer of joy, love, and victory it was," said Ken. "Even Ed expressed his thanks to God saying that at first it was a heavy cross, but now it was a cross of love."

---

* *Prison to Praise*, Merlin C. Carothers, Logos International, 1970.

Later as Janie and Karen guided Ed and the chaplain around the children's home and introduced Ed to the school children, Marilyn requested the children sing something. After a clear sweet presentation of "This is the day the Lord has made: Hallelujah," the children clamored around Ed to touch and meet him personally.

In spite of war and frequent separation from parents, most of the fifty-four children in Vietnam consider themselves highly privileged to have parents who are Wycliffe workers. The small group, after living together in bunkers, over-crowded group housing, and sharing each other's joys and sorrows, know a vanishing experience — the warm security and acceptance of an old fashioned extended family. They have also had the opportunity to meet and know people from other cultures. And in natural everyday occurrences, have learned to trust God for minor and major problems and practice the virtues of truth, tenderness, and compassion.

One of the most striking examples of this came from the school children's acceptance of Ed. Not one child expressed a single thought of revenge. And when one non-missionary child attending the school expressed such a wish, the others, including Linda and David Smith, quickly told him, "You should pray for the soldier, not wish him to jail!"

The proof of their sincerity came when the children began calling Ed, "Uncle Ed" (most WBT children call non-family Wycliffe adults "Uncle" or "Aunt"), and prayed for the "Lord's best help" in his life.

The children were not the only ones praying for the Lord's best for Ed.

"He's a marvellous person," wrote Karen. "In fact the feelings we have for him are unreal. I know if we had to accept and love him out of our own strength we could never do it. But that's not the way it is. God supplies the love and forgiveness and for that I can only praise Him."

After that initial visit with the Smiths, Ed became an accepted member of the Wycliffe family and a much beloved and prayed-for soldier. He received frequent invitations to the Smith's for dinner plus visits from concerned Christian servicemen. Linda Bryant's husband, Bob, had a moment during one dinner evening to present the Four Spiritual Laws and give a casual but clear explanation of the Gospel. For the first time in their lives, Ed and his roommate and companions were face to face with *real* Christianity. "I just can't believe such people exist," said one of Ed's friends.

The Smiths also learned more about Ed. They discovered from his buddies he was not the carousing kind. Rather he liked to stay home and cook steaks for the boys or go to a movie with his roommate. Another said he had an excellent military record and had never known him to get drunk.

Yet in spite of this fine record, Ed knew he might receive a dishonorable discharge and three to six months at hard labor.

In early November Ed received orders to DEROS — immediately return to the States — but legal complications surrounding his pending court martial prevented him from leaving Vietnam. Ken, along with Gene Fuller, another Wycliffe worker, visited Ed to try and cheer him up, but nothing they said or did could bring him out of his dejected discouragement. "Finally," said Ken, "Gene felt led to again share the Gospel with him, making it plain that he should give himself to Christ."

After listening to Gene for a few minutes, Ed said thoughtfully, "Why confess Him when I know I am going to keep on sinning anyway. I know I can't become a good Christian because I don't believe I can give Him all my life."

For the next forty-five minutes they tried to explain to Ed it was God's responsibility to keep him and He would help him live a right kind of life. His responsibility was to take that first step of faith.

"When we left," said Ken, "Ed thanked us and said he understood things more clearly. Then because we knew of Ed's fondness for the Wycliffe school children, we suggested he come to hear them sing during a special evangelistic service the following night."

"My heart was pounding when Ed sat beside us," said Marilyn. "I just felt the Lord was going to work in Ed's heart. I knew many, many people were praying and it seemed the children's songs, the chaplain's comments, and the speaker's message were all directed to Ed."

But Marilyn's hopes were dashed to the ground. As an invitation was given at the conclusion of the service to publicly acknowledge one's faith in Christ, Ed sat in his seat with his head buried in his chest.

After the service Marilyn took the children home and Ken with several others stayed behind to talk with Ed. When the subject of his own personal commitment came up, Ed promptly repeated the same objections he had given to Gene Fuller the day before. After a while, in mild frustration, Ken and the others walked into the annex of the chapel and left Ed and the chaplain alone.

While they waited, Ken commented that Ed was searching but was unable to give himself to the Lord. "Perhaps," someone commented, "he isn't ready yet. The Lord might have to bring him lower ... " As they were about to leave, Chaplain Davis and Ed walked into the annex. Chaplain Davis smiled. "There has been a victory," he said.

Then Ed, with a bright beam on his face, said, "That's right! I finally saw how simple it was and I just had to give myself to Jesus Christ. And now I need to grow, grow, grow."

"It was beautiful," said Ken. "Each man there went up and pumped Ed's hand warmly. And I gave him a hard brotherly hug."

It was late, dark, and raining outside when they left the chapel and someone offered Ed a ride home. "No, thanks," he said. "It's such a *beautiful* night, I'll walk."

# CHAPTER FIVE

## STEP OFF TO A NEW BEGINNING

Ed's new spiritual beginning came through the transforming act of the Holy Spirit. And from the same Holy Spirit's leading came a renewing and enlarged spiritual vision for many of the Smith's friends.

One such friend wrote Marilyn: "I have learned a tremendous truth from the testimony you, Ken, Janie, and Karen have been living, and through Chaplain Davis' sermon the Sunday after Jonny's homegoing. Until this happened I was always afraid of death. But now I have seen the power and victory of the resurrection. In a real way I feel as though I have experienced this power through your lives. It's been a tremendously exciting revelation."

Equally conscious of God's working in her life, Karen Gunnette expressed her feelings of growth in a long tender letter to some of her close friends. " . . . At first it was a difficult time for me. I found it hard to fully accept all God allowed to happen. Two weeks after the accident I sent a tape to my parents telling them the entire story and adding that though I didn't fully understand, I knew the Lord must be *all* to me, or being a Christian was merely words.

"Also in that tape I committed both parents to the Lord. This was the first time in my life I was able to do this. Before I felt my personal need of them too great. But I was willing to give them to the Lord and shift my dependence completely on Him.

"The week I sent the tape I received a letter from my sister telling me Dad was critically ill in the hospital and not expected to live. I was shocked. Within a week I received further word that he had gone to be with the Lord. I could not help thinking of my commitment and how the Lord answered faster than I anticipated.

"What has come out of all these events? It may sound strange, but this tragic accident claiming the life of an innocent child and now the sudden death of my father a few weeks later, has greatly increased my love for God. Let me list some of the reasons.

"First I see only miracles. After seeing the car and how completely demolished it was, I could only whisper, 'Why, why, why had I been saved?' It was totally impossible to understand because I should have been killed. Also the Lord provided all we needed that night and all the nights since. Jonny never felt a thing. He was taken to be with Christ immediately. Praise God! And Ed was shaken deeply enough to search for a personal Christ.

"Also, since the accident so many have seen what Christ means to us. A great number of people have understood that Christ is not something we talk about, but Someone who lives in us.

"And my father? I count it a joy to know my father is with the Lord. I now know death is not the end. It's a step to the real beginning! What eternal joy! Though the past few months have been eventful and sad, they have been overpowering in the knowledge of God's personal existence . . . "

That God was working in extraordinary ways seemed an understatement. Almost every person who was in some way involved with the accident, felt it. After visiting Ed in his barracks one afternoon, an officer handed Ken an envelope with a sympathy card. Ken opened it and found a check for $40.00 with the signatures of five men. "For Jonny's Memorial Fund," it read, "from the men who work with Ed."

Just as Ed's friends felt compelled to do something positive, so Ken felt the Lord leading him to speak out for Ed. When he realized Ed was being detained beyond his normal rotation because of his trial, Ken felt he should visit Ed's commanding colonel. After making an appointment, Ken was ushered into the office of the commanding officer of the 21st Signal Group.

"I sat down with the colonel and his deputy," said Ken. "The colonel sat quietly as I spoke, letting me go into detail about what I wanted them to understand."

Ken explained his conviction that the accident was planned by God and in many ways had accomplished His purposes in many lives. Ken then recounted a number of recent incidents.

"As parent of the child killed in the accident," continued Ken, "I ask that leniency be given Ed in his forthcoming trial."

The colonel and his deputy were overwhelmed and clearly moved with Ken's Christian compassion. He thanked Ken for coming but explained his jurisdiction over the case had been transferred to a Colonel King. Ken left each a copy of the newsletter which had informed their constituency of Jonny's accident, and an appointment was then made for him to see Colonel King.

"If you believe God has been in this from the beginning," said Colonel King after Ken explained his reason for coming, "do you believe God can continue to be in it?" (The colonel referred to Ed's trial over which he would have no power.)

"I do," said Ken.

The colonel then explained how he had requested a special court for Ed because Ed's guilt was not in question. (The doctor's report had established his drunkenness.) "Rather," said the colonel, "the trial will revolve around litigation, character witness, and in this case, the comments of you as parents."

As Ken left, he presented Colonel King with a copy of *Good News for Modern Man*.

After several discouraging delays in Ed's trial date, Marilyn sent a letter of encouragement to Ed's parents.

December 10, 1971

Dear Mr. & Mrs. ---,

Ed is planning to join us for supper again tomorrow night. We hear he likes to cook steaks so have asked him to be our chef. A dear couple will soon be leaving for the States so about twenty of our friends will be here. Ed has joined us here at our missionary group house several times in the past eight weeks. Just recently he has accepted more of our invitations and we are very glad.

You see, we feel God brought Ed into our lives at our Jonny's death. We love Ed and have shared the joy and peace of heart that God has given to us. Our Linda and David have accepted him as their big brother and pray for him as we all do. Our stateside friends who know and support us have prayed for Ed since we told them about Jonny.

On Thanksgiving, Ed, his two roommates, and boss came over for dinner. We have a missionary school here and several teams work in Nha Trang. Sixteen servicemen were also here so we had sixty for dinner. At Christmas time we trust we can make it a joyful time for the fellows again as we remember Jesus' birthday.

We have been wanting to write to assure you of our concern and love for Ed and to tell you he is accepting his extended time here. The delays and problems of the trial can be discouraging, but he feels there is a plan to it all. We know God has planned our lives before we were born and so we love and trust Him.

Most Sincerely,

While Ed waited, the Smiths continued to encourage him in his faith. On several occasions he found it difficult to understand salvation was based not on feelings but on God's eternal promises. Yet he continually stumbled over "not feeling different."

It wasn't until Ken and Marilyn received Ed's Christmas letter that they understood how he truly felt.

15 December 71

Dear Ken and Marilyn,

I just finished reading *When a Child Dies* by Joseph Bayly. I have read it several times since you first gave it to me and each time gained new meaning and understanding. However, the booklet is priceless to me for another reason which I'm certain is quite evident to you and many of your dear friends.

With the Christmas holidays drawing near I have spent many hours trying to decide what I should give you both or what I should do that would in some way repay you for the kindness and love you have given me. From my narrow materialistic viewpoint I decided a monetary gift for your work would be appropriate and beneficial. However, the Lord has shown me the best gift I could possibly give is this letter telling you of the assurance I received today after reading *When a Child Dies*.

When I first learned I was responsible for Jonny's death I was overwhelmed with feelings of sorrow and guilt. I even considered the stupid but seemingly universal solution to problems of such intensity — suicide! But something inside kept telling me this was not the answer.

During the first few days following the accident I wept bitterly — much as Jesus did in the Garden of Gethsemane on the night before He died. I cried to Jesus and demanded to know why He had placed such a heavy cross on my shoulders. That night and most of the next day I continued in my anguish seeking an answer, but no answer came. Gradually after meeting with both of you, Janie, Karen, Chaplain Davis, and with so many of your other Christian friends, the answer began to come. Yet not until today did I feel the answer was complete. You tried to convince me Jonny's death was a blessing from God, not a tragedy. I tried to believe it but I only did it halfheartedly. The sorrow and guilt kept creeping up every time I looked into your eyes, or saw David and Linda. I suppose a certain amount of guilt will remain with me for the rest of my life.

However, this isn't relevant to the point I am trying to make. What I am trying to say is that today after reading *When a Child Dies*, I think I heard Jonny saying to me, "Ed, thank you for bringing death to me. For through death you have given me something much greater than anything you could ever dream of. I am with my Father now and I am happy. I wouldn't want it any other way."

This then, Ken and Marilyn, is my Christmas gift for you. Please share it with whomever you wish.

Sincerely,

(Signed) Ed.

The Smith's 1971 Christmas newsletter briefly described their work in Vietnam and how the Lord continued to be their strength. There were also condensed details of how the Lord worked to bring healing in Ed's life. "Now as Ed talks to us," read the last sentence, "he looks into our eyes!"

# CHAPTER SIX

## A HUNDRED DAYS

The trial was finally set for January 10, 1972 in Cam Ranh. Ed's lawyer, who became so overwhelmed with the Smith's unusual love that he began to rethink his own spiritual position, advised Ed to plead guilty to negligent homicide. And because of this plea, the court proceedings were given to character references. A judge would then decide Ed's sentence.

The trial began at 10:00 A.M, in a quonset hut. The judge sat behind a slightly raised barrier. Ed sat on the left with his counsel. On the right sat the prosecuting attorney; at the back, a recording secretary, and in the center of the room a single chair for the witnesses who were to come in one at a time.

For about thirty minutes Ken and Marilyn sat in the outer office waiting for preliminaries to end and the calling of the first witness. Ken was third.

"What is your name and occupation?" asked the judge.

"Kenneth Smith," answered Ken. "I am a missionary linguist."

"And what is the nature of your work?" asked the lawyer.

Briefly Ken described Wycliffe's linguistic, literacy, and Bible translation goals and his work among the Sedang people.

Ken was then asked if he knew and recognized the accused, and to point him out. After Ken did so he was asked if he had done anything prior to the trial to affect its outcome.

"I sought out Colonel King who initiated the original charges against Ed," said Ken. "And as parent of the deceased, requested any leniency which he could effect."

Ken then told the court, as he had Colonel King, he believed the accident was permitted to bring glory to God. Asked about the nature of Ken's relationship to Ed, Ken described how they first met.

"I requested that Chaplain Davis arrange a meeting with Ed to express our love and forgiveness," said Ken. "My wife and I wanted to assure Ed that we believed God would bring something great out of the accident."

"And," asked the lawyer, "what do you think of the accused as a person?"

"It has been evident to us," said Ken, "Ed is basically an honest person. He has never hesitated to speak the truth when we have spoken about spiritual things. Also when he first came to visit us he was truly repentant, broken, and sincere in his sorrow."

For Ken's last question the lawyer asked him what he would like the outcome of the trial to be.

"I would like the outcome of the trial to be whatever would bring glory to God," said Ken, "and whatever would help Ed grow in his relationship to God."

After Marilyn had been called and was similarily questioned, she and Ken again waited outside. In a few minutes they were joined by the prosecuting lawyer who told them the trial was over and the judge would shortly pronounce the verdict. Ken and Marilyn were invited back inside after Ken asked permission to hear the verdict.

Calling the court back to order the judge asked the defendant and his counsel to stand. "The defendant," said the judge, "is to forfeit one-third of his pay for the next six months. Court adjourned."

On January 25, 1972, Marilyn wrote: "These have been the most glorious 100 days of our whole lives! Psalm 73:25 has been echoing in my heart, 'There is none upon earth that I desire beside Thee.' Our fellowship in our Lord is so close here, but it was gained at the price of our Jonny by His hand of Love.

"And Ed was gained for Jesus, too — praise Him! He left for home Monday and we miss him since he became such a part of our lives as we travailed for his birth and growth in Jesus. This past weekend was so great as he saw God work details for his departure so quickly after the long three-month wait. Sunday was a perfect day as he learned how very much he is loved by all the children and missionaries here. It was so hard for him to leave because he is only beginning to taste life in Christ and fellowship with His own. He is constantly in our prayers."

In her own reflection of the same 100 days, Janie Voss wrote: "I came to Vietnam in my own strength. This has now been changed. I have a peace and rest I never knew before. My basic desire now is just to love people, turn my desires over to the Lord, and let Him have them all."

And Ken wrote about a deep void after Ed left. " . . . Ed was certainly our spiritual son. When he left yesterday, I felt a void that must be filled by God."

God filled Ken's void, only it took a little time! The Smith's January 1973 newsletter told all. " . . . The Jonny Memorial Fund has now risen to over $9,000.00 which covers almost half the cost of the third-floor staff apartments in our new headquarters in Saigon. Praise the Lord!

" . . . At noon this past Thanksgiving day our heavenly Father gave us a special gift. A seven and a half-pound baby was born. We called him Peter *Edward*."

## DATE DUE

| | | |
|---|---|---|
| MAY 02 1995 | | |
| NOV 1 9 1985 | | |
| | | |
| | | |
| | | |
| | | |
| | | |
| | | |
| | | |
| | | |
| | | |
| | | |
| | | |
| | | |
| | | |
| | | |